"The quality of empathic listening that Carl Rogers brought to us decades ago, that unlocks treasures of intimacy, trust, peace and healing, is alive and well in Bill Miller's own unique voice, as he extends the meanings of this vital relational element for today's world. Readily integrated into our everyday lives and the larger cultures of human conflict, my hope is that we choose to live out the delicate yet strong principles of connection that *Listening Well* offers us."

—GAY LEAH BARFIELD
Co-Founder and Former Director, Carl Rogers Institute
for Peace, Center for Studies of the Person, La Jolla, California

"If there ever was a time for *Listening Well*, it is now. In its pages, we learn to use our ears to dissolve differences, open hearts, and build bridges. Nothing more needs saying."

—SCOTT D. MILLER
Director, International Center for Clinical Excellence

"*Listening Well* is a super moon in the dark night sky: brilliant, absorbing, and illuminating. Bill Miller, co-developer of the revolutionary Motivational Interviewing, blends art and science in teaching the quintessential skills of listening and in fostering human connection."

—JOHN C. NORCROSS
Professor of Psychology, University of Scranton

"*Listening Well* is a terrific, hands-on book for individuals or groups dedicated to caring relationships. Full of insight and practical exercises to improve listening skills, I highly recommend it to professionals and lay people alike."

—**DEBRA ENGQUIST**
Retired Pastor

"*Listening Well* is about much more than listening. This short, easy-to-read book provides a brief course in human relationships. With many useful explanations, examples and exercises, the author demonstrates the what, why and how of empathy in human interaction. The book is eminently useful for those who want to or need to improve their listening and relationship skills at work or in personal settings."

—**HOWARD KIRSCHENBAUM**
Former Chair, Counseling and Human Development, University of Rochester

Listening Well

Listening Well

The Art of Empathic Understanding

WILLIAM R. MILLER

WIPF *&* STOCK · Eugene, Oregon

LISTENING WELL
The Art of Empathic Understanding

Wipf & Stock
An Imprint of Wipf and Stock Publishers
199 W. 8th Ave., Suite 3
Eugene, OR 97401

www.wipfandstock.com

PAPERBACK ISBN: 978-1-5326-3484-0
HARDCOVER ISBN: 978-1-5326-3486-4
EBOOK ISBN: 978-1-5326-3485-7

Manufactured in the U.S.A.

With gratitude to Dr. Thomas Gordon

Contents

Preface

Ask most people whether they are a "good listener" and they will say, "Yes." Listening well, however, involves a set of skills that are seldom learned at home or in school, yet are important to the quality of life and relationships. I certainly didn't start out being a good listener, but it is one of the most important things I have learned over time, and I'm still practicing.

There is a lot more involved in listening well than simply keeping quiet (although that can be a good start). This ability was originally called *accurate empathy*[1] and it is more than just feeling for or with someone. It is something that you *do*, an "ability to *perceive and communicate*, accurately and with sensitivity, the feelings of the [person] and the meaning of those feelings."[2]

The good news is that these important skills are learnable; you can get better at them. For five decades I have been helping people to develop their capacity for empathic understanding.[3] I have taught laypeople, individuals and couples in counseling, volunteer and paraprofessional helpers, undergraduate and graduate students, pastors, and professionals in health and social services. You don't need to have a university degree in order to learn this. In fact in our research we have found no relationship between years of education and the ability to use the skills described in this book. Relatively few people pick up these skills in the course of ordinary experience, but they are definitely learnable.

Perhaps the need has never been greater for a rebirth of empathic understanding and lovingkindness in society. The world continues to be torn by inhumanity and conflict. Democratic nations including my own have succumbed to bitter polarization, with few listening to those perceived to be on "the other side." Conflict comes to be viewed as a viable if not essential solution in politics, business, and international relations. Social discourse devolves to increasingly impersonal electronic social media. It need not be so.

The *capacity* for empathic understanding is hardwired in our brains as a potential favoring the survival of individuals and of humankind more generally. Like other talents (such as sports and music), the emergence of this ability depends to some extent on individual capability and also on opportunity for practice.[4] Starting with chapter 5 there are specific "Try It!" opportunities that you can practice to strengthen your skills. Ultimately it's a matter of integrating these skills into your daily life.

Take your time in reading this small book. Yes, there is a big picture to be understood, but there are also specific skills that cannot be learned merely by reading. The components introduced in successive chapters build upon each other, so take the time to practice them as you might if learning to play a musical instrument. Some components may be straightforward and easy for you, things you have already learned about communication. Others may seem simple, but in actual practice turn out to be more challenging. Taken together, they represent a skill that you can continue to refine over the course of a lifetime.

Chapter 1

Together

You never really understand another person until you
consider things from his point of view— until you climb
inside of his skin and walk around in it.

—Harper Lee, *To Kill a Mockingbird*

We are profoundly social creatures. Our language, customs, values,
attitudes, beliefs and even our self-understanding develop from
interacting with others. If someone asks, "Who are you?" much
of the answer is likely to be framed in terms of relationships. You
might describe your family roles, cultural or faith identifications,
vocation or avocations. All of these describe who we are in relation
to others. Even descriptors that imply an absence of relationship
(such as single, independent, solitary, atheist, or self-sufficient)
nevertheless express who and how we are in relation to others.

A wonderful aspect of human nature is that we are not limited to our own experience and perspectives. Books and films give
us access to others' ideas, views, lives, and imagination. Every conversation affords a similar opportunity. We are not restricted to
what we already know, nor required to continue life unaffected and
unchanged by others. We are social beings who are able to benefit
from each other's experience.

The capacity to step out of our own perspective and into another (indeed, the awareness that there *are* realities other than our own) is important in human development. This ability to perceive and identify with another person's perspective is often called *empathy* and is an important part of human intelligence. We can do this even at a simple perceptual level. When you view an object from one side, can you imagine or draw how it might look to someone who is looking at it from the other side? Try it with the two shapes shown below. Can you imagine how these two figures would look when viewed from behind? Some of us are better at this than others, but it is an ability that normally develops as children mature.

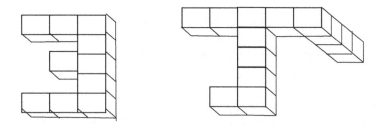

Taking another's perspective moves beyond mere sensory perception to imagining what someone might be thinking or feeling in particular situations. To be moved by a film, book, or play is to put oneself in the position of a character and to feel some of what that person might be experiencing. When listening to people talk, we can imagine what they might be feeling or what else they may be thinking but not saying. Even opponents try to guess what their adversaries are considering.

We are hardwired to do this. "Mirroring" systems in the brain literally duplicate electrical patterns of an action that is observed. Witness or imagine someone lifting a heavy hammer and striking a spike, and your own muscles can subtly tense as if you were doing the movement yourself. Watch someone being gently stroked on the face and the brain area for sensation in that same patch of your own skin shows activation. Some ability to read others' experience and intention is a vital component of social skills and even of survival as an individual and species. People with a relative lack of this ability, as can happen with autism, have profound problems in relating to others. It is built into us to read and guess what other people are thinking and experiencing. It is also clear that our guesses can be wrong, and often are. We can misinterpret someone's intention or misread what they are feeling or meaning. This is where the ability of empathic understanding or *accurate empathy* matters. It is an important skill for life together, and one that you can strengthen with practice. Empathic understanding is not merely something that you *have*, but something that you *do* and *experience*. It happens in relationship and enriches your life. When you develop the needed skills, it is also a precious gift that you can offer to others. It can avert misunderstandings and help your conversations flow more smoothly and easily.

Practicing the skills described in this book can strengthen and deepen everyday relationships with people in your world: with friends and family, co-workers and colleagues, customers or students. Many of the following chapters offer "Try It!" experiences that you can practice to develop your own empathic skills. I suggest that you actually do these exercises, try them out with people who are willing to help you learn, perhaps with someone who would also like to learn. Don't try them at first in the hardest situations, like in the midst of conflict or tension. It is easiest to learn when you are relaxed, your mind is clear, and you can focus on what you are doing. Practice with a goal of *understanding* others and letting them know that you understand. Don't try to make anything happen, except to get better at what you are practicing. You may think of many things that you could say, but focus instead on trying something new and different. Over time the result can be life-changing—it certainly has been for me—but be patient with yourself. Just as in learning to play a sport or a musical instrument, there are some basic skills to master first.

Chapter 2

Accurate Empathy

> [Empathy] is one of the most delicate and powerful ways
> we have of using ourselves. In spite of all that has been
> said and written on this topic, it is a way of being that is
> rarely seen in full bloom in a relationship.
>
> —Carl Rogers, "Empathic: An Unappreciated Way of
>   Being"[5]

To some extent empathy is innate, but accurate empathy is not.
The fact that we can imagine what others are thinking and feeling
does not mean that our guesses are correct. Yet most people most
of the time assume that their interpretations are accurate and they
act accordingly, which can be the source of a great deal of misunderstanding and conflict.

What Empathy is Not

It may be helpful to consider what empathy is by first discuss-
ing what it is not. Empathy (literally *feeling in*) is not the same
as *sympathy*—feeling *for* or pitying someone. Actually, sympathy
involves a certain amount of distancing from the person, backing
away and feeling bad *for* someone else (with emphasis on *else*, an

other). Sympathy is laudable and may motivate compassionate action, but it is not the same thing as empathy. Empathy is also different from *apathy*, the absence of feeling or caring. Apathy implies disconnectedness, a lack of concern or interest. This can be mistaken for objectivity, observing an object without emotional connection. Empathy, in contrast, involves not only attention to but also connecting with the other person, an active interest in understanding what he or she is experiencing. Finally, empathy is not the same thing as *identifying* with a person. It does not require having had similar experience or having a similar feeling at the same time. Empathic understanding with a person who is angry does not require that you simultaneously feel anger yourself. If anything, identifying with someone because of similarity with you can interfere with accurate empathy: what they are expressing lies too close to home for you to understand how it may differ from your own experience.

A Learnable and Useful Skill

Accurate empathy is a learnable skill. It is the ability to understand clearly what other people are experiencing, to "get" them. In his classic novel *Stranger in a Strange Land* Robert Heinlein coined a verb to convey this: I *grok* you. I have a clear sense of what you mean. To be sure, some people do seem to have a head start in developing empathic skill. They pick it up, *grok* it more quickly. Others struggle more at first to set aside their own assumptions and take on another person's perspective. Over the years there have been a few individuals to whom I was unable to teach this skill despite my best efforts. It seemed to be a difficulty in entertaining a perspective other than their own. Most people, however, can gain skill in accurate empathy. Perhaps it is like playing a musical instrument. Some folks just seem to have a natural ear and talent and take to it quickly, whereas a few are truly "tone deaf." In between are many more who can develop reasonable skill and get better over time with practice and coaching. It is also possible to get out of practice with once-learned ability, or at least to neglect using it.

In any event, it is well worth a try. Accurate empathy clarifies communication and strengthens relationships. It can be helpful in parenting, education, friendship, and business. It is also a foundational skill for the helping professions. Developing accurate empathy is a lifelong learning process; with practice you can keep getting better at it.

I hasten to add that there is more here than technique. Although there are specific skills that you can practice in order to become more proficient, empathic understanding over time becomes part of who you *are*. Being open to understanding the experience of others changes you. It is like the difference between practicing an instrument and being a musician.

But we are getting ahead of the story.

Chapter 3

How Accurate Empathy Works

Most people do not listen with the intent to understand; they listen with the intent to reply.

—Steven Covey, *The Seven Habits of Highly Effective People*

In a way, accurate empathy is simple. It's just getting a right understanding of what another person is thinking, feeling, experiencing, and meaning. Someone who is really good at it makes it look easy, but actually it's not, at least not in the beginning. It seems simple until you try it.

One clear and helpful diagram for accurate empathy was provided by Thomas Gordon,[6] a student of the psychologist Carl Rogers whose lifetime of work advanced the understanding of accurate empathy. It consists of just four boxes, as shown in this figure:

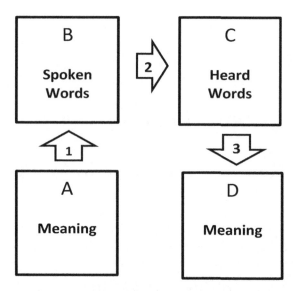

Before someone speaks or otherwise communicates, there is a hidden meaning. It is what is happening in the person's mind and heart at that moment, set against the background of a lifetime of experience. That is Box A on the lower left, marked *Meaning*.

Next there is Box B: what the person says, the *Spoken Words*. If communicating by email or text, the words are all you get. In person, however, we "say" much more than is apparent from the words in a transcript. There is additional information contained in facial expression, vocal tone and volume, posture, and movement. For simplicity the upper-left box refers to "spoken" words, but remember that there is more involved.

Now move over to the right side of the diagram, which represents the listener. A first step is to get the words right, to hear what the speaker actually said (Box C). This is the impressive skill of a court recorder, to set down the exact words as they are spoken. If this is done well an "instant replay" will reproduce accurately what was said. The *Heard Words* are this upper-right box.

Finally there is Box D on the lower right, also labeled *Meaning*. Here the listener interprets what she or he heard. What does the speaker mean? It is always a guess, though often listeners are not conscious that their interpretation is actually a guess, an hypothesis.

There are three places where communication can go wrong, signified by the numbers inside the arrows. Firstly (arrow 1), everyone knows that people don't always say what they mean. In fact, any utterance contains only a small part of the rich inner experience from which it emerged. The speaker may not be good at putting their meaning into words, or might be speaking in a second or third language. Spoken words can be shaped by embarrassment, fear, a desire to make a good impression, or an intention to deceive. The spoken words are but a small part of the story, and that is the first place where clear communication can be derailed.

Secondly (arrow 2), the listener has to hear what was said. This can be hindered by many factors including inattention, distance, distraction, hearing impairment, or listening in what is not your own native language. If the words are not received accurately, then Box C differs from Box B and is another potential source of miscommunication.

The third step (arrow 3) requires decoding what the speaker meant, an abundant source of misunderstanding. The listener quickly (and mostly unconsciously) runs each word through an inner dictionary of possible meanings, and from past experience assembles an interpretation of what was meant. By this time, Box D can be very different from Box A. Yet the listener may respond as though Box D *is* Box A.

Now for an example. Imagine two people who have been living together for a year or so. One of them (Listener) works in an office building, while the other (Speaker) is mostly at home taking care of house and family. The evening meal is over and Speaker has been hoping that they would have some quality time together, though hasn't said so on this occasion. It is disappointing, then, when Speaker sees the partner begin to pack up some materials with the appearance of going back to work, also an unexpressed intention for this evening. So the inner experience (Box A) of the Speaker, who had been hoping for some time together, might be:

"I love you and I really miss our having time together. I was hoping that tonight we could just stay home together and have time to talk and maybe make love."

So how does Speaker put all of this into words? The actual spoken words (Box B) are: "Are you going out?"

It's not too difficult for Listener to hear the words (Box C) even though they weren't looking at each other at that moment. The question resounds in Listener's ear, along with what sounds like a note of irritation in Speaker's tone of voice. Now, it so happens that Listener was raised by rather authoritarian parents and is not quite over rebelling against their control. By virtue of this, what the words mean (Box D) would be: "You should always tell me in advance what you are planning to do and get my permission." Consequently, Listener responds: "Get off my back!"

How very wrong it can go in just one volley! Speaker meant to communicate, "I love you and would like for us to be together," and is astonished to be rebuffed, "Get off my back!" What does it mean? And so the process continues.

Accurate empathy is about closing the loop so that it goes right instead of wrong. At a simplistic level, it is finding out whether Box D is the same as Box A. Did I guess right? Some learnable skills for doing this are described in subsequent chapters, and again they are simple though not necessarily easy. The point here is that accurate empathy involves *finding out* whether your understanding is accurate rather than merely assuming that it is. However, constantly asking, "Do I hear you right that . . . ?" becomes maddeningly annoying and is just not how people normally talk to each other. The art is integrating accurate empathy within the normal flow of conversation, so that Speaker and Listener are aligned. That's what takes real skill.

It is well worth the effort. As the above example illustrates, even a single round from Box A to Box D can go terribly wrong. Clear communication is key in nearly all relationships, a theme that will be explored further in chapters 12 and 13. Once learned, accurate empathy really is a precious gift that you can give to others.

For the speaker, this gift has several important values. First of all, it communicates the listener's caring and respect even without directly saying it: "*You matter to me. I want to understand what you mean and am willing to take the time to know you better. What you say and mean is important to me.*" Secondly, it helps the speaker feel heard and understood. There is no need to keep saying the same thing over and over again because the listener clearly gets it. And at least as important is a third value, that it helps speakers explore and more clearly understand their own experience. In fact, accurate empathy is a skill that counselors learn precisely for this reason. The gift is also valuable to the giver. For the listener it can head off misunderstandings and deepen relationships. I believe that practicing accurate empathy over time also changes the listener. With ability in empathic understanding can come greater acceptance, compassion, forgiveness, and humility. It is an ever present reminder that you are not the center of the universe, the sole source of truth. Accurate empathy opens your awareness of both the diversity and the interconnectedness of human beings. At least that has been my experience.

Chapter 4

The Attitude of Empathic Understanding

What most people really need is a good listening to.

—Mary Lou Casey

Like music, empathic understanding involves more than technique. To be sure there are component skills that can be improved through practice, but technique is not the heart of the matter. Good listening is like putting on a particular hat, an empathic attitude, and accepting a specific role. There is a mindset or "heartset" with which one enters into a conversation when practicing accurate empathy. This is not a prerequisite before you begin to practice. If anything, the practice of accurate empathy teaches you these habits of mind and heart. You do need at least a willingness, though, an openness to the assumptions behind empathic understanding.

A first assumption is that it is valuable to see through another's eyes, to "walk in their shoes," to understand what they perceive and experience. This actually *is* a prerequisite to clear communication, to realize that your guesses are incomplete at best. At the very least, don't respond until you are sure that you understand.

Second, there is a willingness not to be the center of attention. To be empathic is to step away from self-centeredness, to temporarily suspend your own "stuff" in the service of understanding. Empathic understanding involves a genuine interest in and curiosity about the experience of others. One of the great privileges I have enjoyed as a psychologist is that of being admitted to the private inner world of so many different people over time. That joy is not restricted to professional helpers. It can and should be shared by friends and lovers. It can be an important part of education, leadership, ministry, and mentoring. It can enrich relationships with family members and coworkers.

Listening beyond oneself brings the discovery of wisdom in others. Here is a third mindset: that other people have much to teach us, especially those who are different from us in important ways. Empathic understanding involves respecting and valuing differences and learning from them.

Beneath accurate empathy at a deeper level is compassion as an intention and habit of the heart. Compassion goes beyond mere interest in or curiosity about others. It is a desire for and commitment to their well-being. The more you understand another's suffering, the more you long to lighten it.[7] The more you listen deeply to others, the more you sense how alike and interconnected we are.

Willingness to see through another's eyes, to suspend self-centeredness, to receive respectfully what they have to offer, and to desire their well-being—these are habits of mind and heart that underlie and motivate empathic understanding.

Chapter 5

Roadblocks to Listening

> We have two ears and one mouth and we should use them proportionally.
>
> —Susan Cain, *Quiet: The Power of Introverts in a World That Can't Stop Talking*

One way to understand something is first to know what it is not. Although most of us believe that we are good listeners, what we actually do in conversations is quite a different matter.

Here again I borrow from the writings of Thomas Gordon to describe what the practice of good listening is not. [8] I have somewhat revised the twelve roadblocks that he described, but the wisdom and simplicity are his. They are twelve ways in which people often respond instead of listening well, sometimes even with the intention of being a good listener.

1. *Directing* is telling someone what to do, as if giving an order or a command.

    - You've got to face up to reality!
    - Knock it off!
    - Go right back there and tell her you're sorry!
    - Stop complaining and do something about it!

2. *Warning* involves pointing out the risks or dangers of what a person is doing. This can also be a threat.

    • If you do, you'll be sorry.

    • Don't you know what's going to happen if you keep this up?

    • You're going to destroy this relationship.

    • You'd better listen to me.

3. *Advising* includes making suggestions and providing solutions, usually with the intention of being helpful.

    • Here's what I would do if I were you . . .

    • Have you thought about . . . ?

    • One thing you could try is . . .

    • How about . . . ?

4. *Persuading* can be lecturing, arguing, giving reasons, or trying to convince with logic.

    • If you just think about it you'll realize that . . .

    • Yes, but don't you see that . . .

    • Now let's think this through. The facts are . . .

    • It's the right thing to do, and here's why . . .

5. *Moralizing* is telling people what they *should* do.

    • You really should . . .

    • You need to . . .

    • I think you ought to . . .

    • It's your duty to . . .

6. *Judging* can take the form of blaming, criticizing, or simply disagreeing.

- Well, it's your own fault!
- You're still asleep at ten o'clock in the morning?
- No, you're wrong about that.
- Well, what did you expect?

7. *Agreeing* usually sounds like taking sides with the person, perhaps approving or praising.

- Yes, you're absolutely right.
- Good for you!
- That's what I would do, too.
- You're such a good mother.

8. *Shaming* or ridiculing can include attaching a name or stereotype to what the person is saying or doing.

- That's a silly way to think.
- How could you do such a thing?
- You really ought to be ashamed of yourself.
- You're being so selfish!

9. *Analyzing* offers a reinterpretation or explanation of what the person is saying or doing.

- You don't really mean that.
- Do you know what your real problem is?
- You're just trying to make me look bad.
- I think what's actually going on here is . . .

10. *Probing* asks questions to gather facts or press for more information.

- When did you first realize that?
- What makes you feel that way?

- Where was the last place you saw it?
- Why?

11. **Reassuring** can sound like sympathizing or consoling.

- Oh, you poor thing. I'm sorry for you.
- There, there— I'm sure this will all work out.
- Things aren't really so bad.
- You'll probably look back on this in a year and laugh.

12. **Distracting** tries to draw people away from what they are experiencing by humoring, changing the subject, or withdrawing.

- Let's talk about something else.
- Oh, aren't you the gloomy one! Lighten up.
- You think you've got problems. Let me tell you . . .
- That reminds me of a joke.

So What's the Problem with Roadblocks?

Sometimes when I describe these as roadblock responses people ask, "What's wrong with that?" Actually I'm not saying that these responses are wrong. There are times and places where each of these might be appropriate. It's just that they are not good listening, and if you want to develop accurate empathy skills it's important to suspend these reflexive ways of responding. Roadblocks tend to divert people from their natural flow of experience. The speaker must go around the roadblock in order to keep on exploring in the same direction, which can be diverting.

There are also some implicit themes behind roadblock responses that get in the way of understanding. Intended or not, many of them take a one-up position: "I know best. Listen to me." Some of them are outright put-downs implying that there is something wrong with the speaker, and that tends to shut down communication. Others such as agreeing, reassuring, and distracting are mostly conversation stoppers: "You've said enough now." It's not that you should *never* respond in these ways. It's just that they are not good listening when the purpose is to understand the person's perspective and experience.

Try It!

It doesn't take long to experience the limitations of roadblock responses. As with most of the exercises suggested in this book, you will need at least one practice partner. For this exercise there is a Speaker and a Helper. The Speaker's task is to discuss something about yourself that you might like to improve, some positive change you might want to make in your daily life. The whole conversation should take about five minutes. Start by describing briefly what change you are considering.

The Helper's role is to interject within five minutes as many of the roadblock responses as possible. Keep the list of roadblocks handy. Each one can be short and sweet:

- Judging: You really should do that. You need to.
- Agreeing: Yes, you're right
- Interpreting: I don't think that's your real problem . . .
- Suggesting: Here's how you could do it . . .

Have some fun with this. It doesn't need to be deadly serious, just try to keep going. Speaker, try to keep talking about what you might change. Helper, keep inserting different roadblocks. If the conversation breaks down into hilarity, the point is made. Switch roles if you wish and try it again.

Chapter 6

The Picture Without the Sound

Never miss a good chance to shut up.

—Will Rogers

Even without making a sound there are ways to communicate whether you are listening and understanding. Imagine a video screen on which you are watching two people in a conversation, but with the sound turned off. Even without seeing whose lips are moving, how can you know when one of them is listening, and tell how well they are following what the other person is saying? In other words, what does a good listener look like? The answer can vary some from culture to culture. For example, there are noticeable cultural differences in how close or far back listeners might stand when in conversation, and in how readily they touch the speaker. So keep these differences in mind as I describe signs of listening, particularly if you live in a culture very different from American and European contexts.

The key here is to show that you are giving your undivided attention. One reasonably consistent signal that you are listening has to do with the eyes. When attending well a listener typically maintains fairly constant eye contact, whereas the speaker normally fluctuates between looking the listener in the eyes and looking away. Even here there are cultures and contexts in which it is more respectful for the listener not to stare but instead to look down. You will know from your own experience how to signal good attending in your own culture, but a common practice is to maintain eye contact when you are the listener. The speaker can comfortably look away and break eye contact—that is, unless you are sitting or standing directly face to face, literally *confronting* each other.

How else can you convey good listening without making sounds? Is it better to keep an objective "poker face" without much facial change? There are contexts (like poker) in which that can be appropriate, but usually an engaged listener will show variations in facial expression that in part mirror what the speaker is saying. Mismatches can reflect inattention: Smiling is odd when the speaker is talking about something very sad. Occasional nods (but not constant bobbing) of the head can convey understanding. Posture communicates interest and attention— turning toward or away, leaning in or back.

Good listening is also signaled by what you are *not* doing. Empathic listeners are not interrupting, looking around for someone more interesting, or checking their watches and fiddling with their electronic devices. Think about how you can tell from the picture without the sound whether a listener is interested or would rather be doing something else.

Then there are those vocal sounds that are not quite words, though they can be spelled out: Uh huh. Hmm. Mm hmm. Ah! A gasp. A sigh. In Scandinavia and the Canadian Maritimes one hears people draw in breath with a "Yah" kind of sound to signal listening or agreement (though they would not answer a question this way), analogous to how others may use "mm hmm." These little vocalizations say, "I hear you." "I'm with you." "Tell me more."

Try It!

You can practice this in a way that increases awareness of the dynamics of listening. Work with a partner where one of you, the Speaker, is prepared to talk about a topic in monologue fashion for about three minutes. Some possible topics are:

- What it was like growing up in my home
- My favorite (or dream) vacation
- An experience I had that might be difficult for others to understand.

The Listener's role is to show that you are listening, interested, and understanding without using any words or even making vocalizations like those described above. How can you demonstrate listening without making a sound? How can you show nonverbally that you are accurately understanding what the Speaker is saying? If you wish, switch roles and try it again. Discuss the experience of being the Speaker and Listener during this exercise.

Chapter 7

Asking Questions

The important thing is not to stop questioning. Curiosity has its own reason for existence.

—Albert Einstein, *Old Man's Advice to Youth*

Now that you've practiced listening without using words (chapter 6), it's time to turn up the sound that goes with the picture. Often the first thing that occurs to a listener is to ask questions. That's what an interviewer does, after all. Reporters have a list of questions to which they want answers.

There is indeed room for asking questions within the world of accurate empathy, but there are also important limitations. For one thing, as discussed in chapter 5, asking questions is not the same thing as listening. In fact it can be a roadblock because you are directing the person's attention toward topics of particular interest to you rather than just listening with acceptance. Most people do ask far too many questions when trying to be a good listener, and breaking the habit of over-relying on questions is part of developing accurate empathy. Too many questions can feel like interrogation. A simple guideline is not to ask three questions in a row.

Yet there is definitely a role for questions. A well-asked question can invite a conversation and open the door so you can follow with good listening. A question can help to clarify something that you don't understand.

There is a difference between open and closed questions. Closed questions invite a short answer, asking for specific information and thereby limiting the person's options in answering. Some simple examples of closed questions are:

- What is your address? (Fact gathering)
- Do you smoke? (Yes or no)
- Do you prefer coffee or tea? (Multiple choice)
- Don't you think you should cut down? (Rhetorical— a preferred answer is implied)

Closed questions are more controlling, and a series of these puts the speaker into a passive role. Sometimes the unspoken implication is that "When I have asked enough questions, then I'll have the answer for you."

Open questions, in contrast, open the door for a wide range of possible answers. Some examples:

- How has your week been?
- What is a typical day like for you?
- Tell me about your family when you were growing up.
- What's troubling you?

You can see that even open questions still limit the topic of conversation somewhat, but at least they are a starting point. After asking an open question like this, try just listening rather than following up with more questions, and see where the conversation goes without your steering it.

Often listeners ask too many questions because they don't know what else to do. If all of the "roadblocks" in chapter 5 are not listening, then what is left? That's the subject of chapter 8.

Try It!

Meanwhile, have some fun with this practice exercise in which you rely on asking closed questions. This is a foundation on which you can build in the next chapter. It works well with three or four people, though two can do it. Take turns being the Speaker, whose task is to say, "One thing that you should know about me is that I am _____." Fill in the blank with one adjective that describes you and that leaves some room for interpretation. Some possible examples: I am persistent caring stubborn faithful patient creative curious compassionate adventuresome.

The task of the Listener(s) is to guess what the Speaker means, and to do so in a particular format that is a bit like the "Twenty Questions" game. As a Listener, ask yourself, "What *might* that word mean about the person? Ask only closed questions to which the answer is "Yes" or "No", using these exact words: "Do you mean that you _____?" The Speaker in turn is allowed to answer *only* "Yes" or "No", without any further elaboration. Here's how it might sound:

> Speaker: One thing you should know about me is that I am untraditional.
>
> Listener 1: Do you mean that you have no traditions in your family?
>
> Speaker: No.
>
> Listener 2: Do you mean that you tend to be unpredictable?
>
> Speaker: (Pauses) No.
>
> Listener 3: Do you mean that you like to follow your own path?
>
> Speaker: Yes.
>
> Listener 2: Do you mean that you don't like people telling you what to do?
>
> Speaker: Yes.

Listener 1: Do you mean that you want to be independent, with no one relying on you?

Speaker: No.

And so it goes. Ask closed questions until you think you have a
good sense of what the Speaker may mean or until you give up.
Then give the Speaker a moment to clarify what he or she really did
and didn't mean. Then someone else becomes the Speaker. This is
somewhat easier if there are two or more Listeners to take turns
coming up with questions.

Several insights often emerge from this exercise. First, good
guesses are often wrong. What seems to be an obvious implication
may not be at all what the Speaker means. It can feel frustrating
for the Listener to be limited to closed questions. That's the challenge of a "Twenty Questions" game. Also the Speaker usually feels
frustrated to be limited to just "Yes" or "No", and wants to say more
in order to be understood. Speakers often try to convey more by
the *way* in which they say "Yes" or "No", particularly through voice
inflections. The good news is that you will be freed from these
limitations in chapter 8.

Chapter 8

Forming Reflections

Listening is not merely not talking, though even that is
beyond most of our powers; it means taking a vigorous,
human interest in what is being told us. You can listen
like a blank wall or like a splendid auditorium where
every sound comes back fuller and richer.

—Alice Duer Miller

It is fitting that this chapter lies near the center of this book because
now we are getting into the heart of the matter with the foundational skill of forming reflective listening statements. Empathic
understanding involves more than this, but reflective listening is a
solid path that can lead you in the right direction. It is a skill that
you can continue to hone over time and can help you become a
more empathic person. It is a *doing* path toward *being*.

Reflective listening[9] requires the skills already discussed, of
refraining from roadblocks (chapter 5) and giving your undivided
attention (chapter 6). This can be challenging enough in itself. Carl
Rogers observed that "Apparently the act of attending carefully to
another person is a difficult task for most people. They are usually thinking what they will say when the speaker stops. Or they
focus on some specific point made by the speaker and then fail to

attend to the rest because they are thinking up arguments against the specific point."[10]

So what exactly is reflective listening? Just like the "Do you mean that . . . ?" questions of chapter 7, a reflection makes a guess about what the speaker means. However a good reflection is not phrased as a question but as a *statement*. That requires at least two specific changes in language. First, you eliminate any front-end words that mark it as a question: "Do you . . . " "Are you . . . " "Is it . . . ", and so on. Thus from the question "Do you mean that you are talented?" you would drop the words, "Do you mean that," leaving only, "You are talented?" However that's still a question. The other change is to get rid of that question mark at the end. When speaking English and most other European languages the difference is to inflect your voice *down* rather than *up* at the end of the sentence. Try it. Note the difference in spoken words between:

> You are talented?   and   You are talented.
>
> You're unhappy?   and   You're unhappy.

It has to do with how you use your voice.

So in order to turn a question into a reflection, remove the question words and also inflect your voice downward at the end so that it is a statement instead of a question. If you're having trouble coming up with a reflective statement, you can start out by first thinking the question (Do you mean that you . . .) and then make those two changes. Just start with "You" and turn your voice down at the end. Good reflective listening is more complex than this, but it's a head start.

It usually feels strange at first to be making a statement rather than asking a question. After all, you know that what you are saying is a guess, so shouldn't you be asking instead of telling? Isn't that putting words in the person's mouth? What if your guess were wrong? Something in you mightily wants to turn the inflection up at the end to make it a question. Trust me that it's usually better to use the form of a statement when reflecting, even though it feels odd to you at first.

Here is one reason why. Linguistically a question places a demand on the person for an answer. It is a subtle pressure, a micro-interrogation. Statements typically don't have that effect. Suppose for example that someone were expressing some frustrations to you about a conversation with her mother. Speak these two lines aloud as a listener:

> You're angry with your mother?

> You're angry with your mother.

It's all in the inflection of the voice, and there are many different ways to read these lines. Can you sense a subtle difference, though, in how the speaker may respond depending on whether you ask a question or make a statement? There is just something about a question that often makes the speaker want to take it back, or at least have second thoughts about whether she should have said it.

Now imagine that you're talking to a teenager who has misbehaved in some way. Speak these two lines aloud as a listener:

> You don't see anything wrong with what you did?

> You don't see anything wrong with what you did.

Can you feel the difference? Somehow the question implies that the person *should* see something wrong, even if that's not your intention. The statement does not have this connotation, inviting the person to respond more honestly and less defensively. A statement usually sounds more accepting, whereas questions using the same words can feel judgmental.

What happens when you offer a reflective listening *statement*? Typically the speaker keeps right on talking, moving along the same road without having to dodge a roadblock. Reflective listening allows people to express and explore their own experience without interference. In this way, the art of empathic understanding is sacrificial; for the time being, at least, you are suspending your own "stuff," the opinions and judgments and suggestions discussed as roadblocks in chapter 5. Your whole focus is to listen to and understand the inner experience of this speaker. As I've said before, that is also a benefit for you the listener as a privileged visitor to another's inner world. When you visit someone else's home there is no need to rearrange the furniture. Just sit and listen.

But what happens if you guess wrong? Reflection is one skill in which there is no penalty for missing. People just tell you what they *do* mean. Thus over time you get better at guessing because every time you offer a reflection you receive immediate feedback.

Here is how a conversation might flow with the Listener relying entirely on reflective listening. The starting point is the same one used in chapter 7.

> Speaker (S): One thing you should know about me is that I'm nontraditional.
>
> Listener (L): You don't have any traditions in your family. (An incorrect guess)
>
> S: Well, actually we do. That's not what I mean. I just don't like doing things the way people expect me to.
>
> L: It has something to do with expectations, with what other people want you to do.
>
> S: Right! I mean why should I be what somebody else wants me to be?
>
> L: That doesn't make any sense to you, trying to please someone else.
>
> S: Yes. I want to be who I am. Now, sometimes it is reasonable for people to have expectations of me.
>
> L: Expectations that are acceptable to you.
>
> S: Sure. You don't go into a committed relationship without having some expectations of each other. That's reasonable. Or in a job, I guess.
>
> L: When you love or work for someone it's reasonable for them to have some expectations of you.
>
> S: Yeah. I would rather work for myself, but that's reality.

L: So it's kind of like a balance between being your own person and being with other people who do have some reasonable expectations of you.

S: A balance, yes. I mean, I don't like being accountable to other people I guess, but nobody is an island as they say.

How much farther, faster, and deeper a conversation can go when the listener takes time to offer good reflections instead of relying on questions! The dialogue flows better because speaker and listener are aligned. It's likely that in this conversation the speaker is also reflecting on and gaining a better understanding of his or her own meaning and experience.

Notice something else about this conversation. The reflections offered by the listener don't interrupt or derail the speaker. Neither is the listener merely parroting what the speaker has said. The reflections move the conversation forward without jumping too far. I have called this form of reflection, "continuing the paragraph." Instead of repeating what a speaker just said, the listener is offering what might be the *next* sentence in the paragraph. After the Listener's first miss in the conversation above, the words could be rewritten as a single paragraph spoken by the Speaker just by changing a few pronouns. That's an artful form of reflective listening that can make the river of conversation flow more smoothly and rapidly.

Try It!

Here's a next step to try in practicing the art of reflective listening. The format and the people can be the same as the exercise in chapter 7, but this time there are important differences. As before, the Speaker says, "Something you should know about me is that I am _____," ending with an adjective that is open to interpretation. This time, however, the Listener(s) will offer reflections instead of questions. If you feel stuck as a Listener, first think of a "Do you mean that you . . . ?" question, then remove the question words and start with "You," inflecting your voice downward at the end to make it a statement. Take your time and be patient; it takes a while to get used to reflecting in this way.

And, by the way, the Speaker is now freed to respond however feels natural. If you're the Speaker don't just answer "Yes" or "No," but say more about what you mean. If the Listener asks you a question (even by inflecting upward), don't respond. Wait until it is a reflective listening statement and then reply.

That makes it all the more challenging for the Listener(s) who now must remember and reflect not only the Speaker's original statement but also the new information coming in after each reflection. Got the idea? The example earlier in this chapter shows how this exchange can flow, but there's no telling what direction your own conversation will take. Offer reflections until you feel satisfied that you understand what the Speaker means, then switch roles.

Here are some common experiences when people try this exercise. First, reflecting is hard! It feels so much easier to ask questions. Listeners also think of all the things they might have said instead of reflecting (many of which are roadblocks). Speakers often enjoy the exercise. After all, how many conversations do you have in the course of a typical month in which the listener has no focus other than to understand well what you mean? Sometimes even speakers are surprised by where the conversation goes, discovering meanings of which they were not initially aware.

Chapter 9

Diving Deeper

It takes two to speak the truth—one to speak and another to hear.

—Henry David Thoreau

In the classic joke a lost stranger goes up to a New Yorker on the street and asks, "How do I get to Carnegie Hall?" The answer: "Practice, practice, practice."

So it is with accurate empathy. The more you work on developing a listening mindset and practicing the skill of reflective listening, the more natural it becomes. A real advantage for learning is that every time you offer a reflection you receive immediate feedback about its accuracy. Whether the basic reply is "Yes" or "No," in either case you learn more about what the person actually does mean. Over time, you just get better at guessing and more skillful in reflecting meaning. Sometimes when I offer a reflection the person asks me, "How did you know that?" The answer is: "Practice, practice, practice."

As introduced in chapter 8, skillful reflective listening is not just repeating back what you hear. Merely repeating what a person says (sometimes called a *simple* reflection) sounds odd and usually doesn't seem to go anywhere:

Speaker: I had a pretty rough day today.

Listener: You had a rough day.

S: Nothing seemed to go right.

L: Sounds rough.

S: Yeah.

L: Things just didn't go well for you.

S: Right.

This doesn't sound much like a normal conversation and the Listener hasn't learned very much about the Speaker's day. The problem here is that the Listener is staying *too* close to the Speaker's words.

More skillful reflections take a small risk, offering a guess about what the Speaker may mean but hasn't quite said. It really is like continuing the paragraph, guessing what might be the *next* sentence. What *might* the Speaker mean by saying, "I had a pretty rough day today"? It could mean:

- I got into a conflict with someone.
- I had some unpleasant experiences.
- I worked hard.
- I'm really tired.
- I feel sad (or discouraged, or maybe angry).

Reflective listening is about making a guess (sometimes called *complex* reflection) based on what you see, hear, and know so far. It doesn't matter if your initial guess is right or wrong. Either way you will both probably learn more.

Speaker: I had a pretty rough day today.

Listener: You do look tired.

S: I am. Nothing seemed to go right today.

L: Sounds like it wasn't just one thing that happened.

S: Well, mostly I got into it with my boss at work. He started criticizing me again and I told him he was being unfair and it all went downhill from there.

L: You're worried about your job.

S: Not really. I don't think he'd sack me or anything, but I'm just tired of him finding fault with me all the time.

L: Like he's picking on you.

S: Oh, I don't know. He's pretty hard on everybody lately.

L: And that's what doesn't seem right to you.

S: I just don't look forward to going to work anymore.

L: You used to enjoy your job, but it's soured a bit.

S: Actually I still enjoy what I do, and I think I do good work. It's just that I don't feel appreciated.

Every one of the Listener's responses in this example is a reflective listening statement. Each one makes a guess about what the Speaker might mean. Notice how the conversation continues to flow. Again it's almost like a single paragraph, even when the guess is wrong.

A good reflection continues the story. Instead of merely rehashing what was said, you want to move the story forward. That in part is why it flows like a good conversation; you are helping the speaker continue the story instead of just echoing or placing roadblocks. There are several reflections in the above example where the Listener's guess isn't quite on the mark, but they quickly realign and the story proceeds anyhow.

It takes practice for reflective listening to begin feeling comfortable and natural, but there are good reasons to persist in your learning. Reflective listening conveys respect, helps to prevent misunderstanding, and can strengthen relationships. Remember the four-box diagram from chapter 3? Instead of assuming that his or her interpretation (Box D) is right, the listener checks it against the speaker's own meaning (Box A). Thus reflective listening closes the communication loop so that the listener gradually comes to have more accurate understanding, better grasping the speaker's inner meaning and experience.

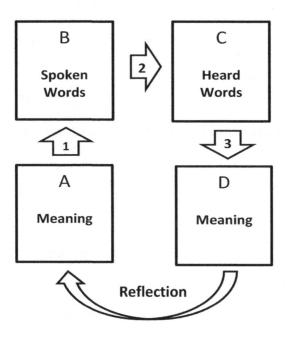

Accurate empathy also broadens your own perspective by sharing in the life experience of others. It is a foundation for deeper understanding and trust within family and friendship. Such deep listening truly is a gift, and one for which many people are hungry.

Accurate Empathy and Reflective Listening

This is a good place to clarify the difference between reflective listening and accurate empathy. Reflective listening as described in this book is a particular practice, a learnable skill for improving your understanding of another person's meaning. It is something that you *do*. Empathic understanding or accurate empathy is more a way of *being* that emerges over time, and includes the underlying attitude described in chapter 4. You develop accurate empathy with and for people by taking the time to listen deeply and understand layers of meaning and feeling that they are willing to share with you. It moves sensitively beyond superficial relationship toward understanding and even intimacy. Empathic understanding is an accepting and compassionate way of being with people that invites openness.[11] Reflective listening is a particular practice that fosters empathic understanding.

Reflections can be intermixed with questions, and usually are. Because asking questions often feels so much easier than empathic listening, the challenge is to not ask too many questions and to rely instead on reflections. Remember that turning your voice up at the end of a statement turns it into a question. Try asking an open question (chapter 7) and then following up with at least two reflections as you listen to the person's reply.

Fine Tuning: Choosing Your Words

Understating and Overstating

Whenever you offer a reflective listening statement you are making choices about the particular words to use. Some words reflect the *intensity* of what the speaker is saying, and it is possible to either overstate or understate it. Certain words imply lower intensity:

- That seems *a bit* unfair to you.
- You're *somewhat* upset about it.
- You *kind of* doubt whether he's telling you the truth.
- You're *a little* nervous about what's going to happen.

Other words that can be used in reflections are amplifiers:

- You are *very* sure about that.
- There has been *a lot* of chaos in your life lately.
- You're *really* suspicious.

- There's *definitely* no way that will work.

Intensity in reflection also has to do with the particular nouns, verbs, or adjectives that you use. Consider the example of words about anger. There are smaller words like *irritated* or *annoyed*; medium anger words like *angry* and *mad*; and great big words like *fuming, irate, furious,* and *enraged*. As you can imagine, it does matter which words you choose. If you overstate a feeling, the speaker is more likely to back away from it.

> Speaker: I can't believe how unfair my boss is being.
>
> Listener: You're *enraged* about this.
>
> S: Well no, not enraged. I'm not really all that angry about it.

On the other hand, understating is more likely to encourage the person to continue expressing.

> S: I can't believe how unfair my boss is being.
>
> L: You're *a little annoyed* about this.
>
> S: Annoyed? I'm really angry about it! This has been going on way too long.

As a general guideline, if you want the person to continue expressing, lean toward understating.

Analogies

Another artful way to express understanding is to offer an analogy that compares the person's experience to something that it's *like*. One such figure of speech, a *simile,* contains words such as "like" or "as though" to show the connection or comparison that you are making:

> You feel as though the walls are closing in on you.
>
> It's like you suddenly saw the light.

This can be particularly effective if you use analogies from the person's own experience. Someone from a farm might understand what it means to be "blown around like a weathervane," a comparison that could be lost on a city dweller who has never seen a weathervane.

> Speaker: I feel so confused. When I'm around my parents I'm one kind of person. When I'm with my friends I tend to go along with whatever they want. I want people to like me and accept me, but I don't really know who I am.
>
> Listener: You're a bit like a weathervane, turning whichever way the wind is blowing.

I was listening once to a musician from a symphony orchestra, who was talking about feeling lonely and empty. "It's like the sound of a flute in an empty concert hall," I said. "Yes, exactly!" he replied, and broke into tears.

The Music

Finally, it matters not only what you say, but how you say it. This is the music of speech, and it can give very different meanings to the very same words. As discussed in chapter 8, intonation makes the difference between a statement and a question:

> You're angry with your mother. (Gently)
>
> You're angry with your mother? (Incredulous)

Also in the music is where emphasis is placed:

> *You* are afraid of him.
>
> You *are* afraid of him!
>
> You are *afraid* of him.
>
> You are afraid of *him*?

Sarcasm, skepticism, or suspicion can easily creep into the music, and people tend to be quite attuned to hearing such overtones, even if unconsciously. Can you speak these same words:

"So it's not your fault. You really had nothing to do with it."

in different ways that convey (1) sympathy, (2) mistrust, (3) sarcasm, or (4) disgust? Try it!

These are subtleties—intensity, analogy, voice tone—and trying to consciously attend to them all can actually distract you from good listening. What will keep you on the right track is the mindset and heartset beneath your listening (chapter 4). When you know that you are making a guess, your reflective listening statement still has a tentative tone, quite different from the music if you were insisting that your interpretation is correct. When you listen with curiosity, compassion, patience, and a genuine desire to understand, you're unlikely to stray far from the path.

Try It!

A good next step is to get some practice in trusting and relying on reflections. It's a bit like practicing scales when learning a musical instrument. Sustained practice helps to make a skill more automatic. Work with a partner who is willing to talk to you about a personally meaningful topic for five to ten minutes and also to be patient with you while you practice reflective listening. Here are some possible topics for a Speaker:

- Describe each of your parents and your relationship with them when you were growing up.

- Explain how you became interested and involved in the work that you are doing now.

- Talk about a favorite person who had a particularly important impact on your life. What was that person like, and what positive effect(s) did she or he have on you?

If you're the Speaker, pause often to give the Listener a chance to practice reflection. It can take a little while for the Listener to form a good reflection, so don't just keep on talking. Be patient with some silence to give the Listener time and space to reflect.

When you're the Listener, it may be tempting to ask questions. Try instead to offer reflective listening statements. It's OK to ask an open question here and there, but offer at least two reflections for every question that you ask. If there are three of you practicing, one might be an observer by counting questions and reflections. When the story seems complete and you have an understanding of the Speaker's experience, you can switch roles if you wish. Here is how such a conversation might begin:

> Listener: So what do you want to talk about?
>
> Speaker: I think I'll tell you about someone who really influenced me. His name was George.
>
> L: He was someone important to you. (A reflection, resisting the temptation to ask questions)
>
> S: He still is. He was a teacher who really believed in me.
>
> L: He saw something in you. (Reflection)
>
> S: Exactly! He treated me with respect, and had a good sense of humor.
>
> L: How could you tell that he respected you? (Open question)
>
> S: I guess it was the way he talked to me. He never talked down to me, and he was interested in what I thought about things.
>
> L: More like a friend. (Reflection)
>
> S: He was friendly, sure, but not like buddy-buddy. I knew he had a lot to teach me.
>
> L: You respected him, too. (Reflection)
>
> S: Definitely. I couldn't believe he took so much extra time outside of class just to talk to me, and I think I

learned as much in those chats in his office as in class. Maybe more.

L: You were worth talking to. (Reflection)

S: That's how I felt. He didn't have to be interested in me, but he was. He took the time, and he didn't just want me to memorize whatever he said in class and spit it back. He wanted me to think about it, and was interested in what I thought.

L: How did that affect you? (Open question, but could have made a guess instead in the form of a reflection)

S: I guess he helped me feel smart, like I had something to contribute and wasn't just a receptacle.

This is just a beginning, but it illustrates how open questions and reflections help the conversation to flow. In each case where the Listener asked a question it could have been a reflection instead, and of course the Listener could have been asking questions instead of reflecting. Do practice offering reflective listening statements rather than questions, even though asking questions probably feels easier.

Chapter 10

Affirming

Hold on to what is good, even if it is a handful of earth.

—A Pueblo Blessing

This chapter describes another practice that is helpful in building and strengthening relationships. It is the habit of seeing and affirming what is good in others.

To affirm what is good requires first that you *notice* it. There is an odd attraction to negativity. If I receive a hundred evaluation forms from a class or workshop, the vast majority are usually quite positive, but then there will always be a few from folks who found the experience less helpful and point to faults and what could be improved. I am still tempted to leaf quickly through the many positive comments and dwell on the negative critiques. In coaching there is a similar temptation to focus on what the learners are doing wrong that needs improvement, while glossing over all that they did well. Even the evening news fixates on the darker side of nature and human nature.

An antidote to this negativity bias is to develop a habit of noticing and appreciating what is good, consciously and conscientiously to catch people doing something well. Affirming can involve recognizing and commenting on someone's strengths, efforts, steps in the right direction, or best intentions. It need not be something large or grand and it should always be genuine, not manufactured or exaggerated. Ways of doing this appropriately do vary across cultures, but most people are hungry for affirmation precisely because so many of us are stingy with it. Affirmations might also be:

- An expression of good wishes (I hope this weekend goes well for you!)
- Appreciation or affection (You're a good friend.)
- Gratitude (Thanks for listening to me!)

To affirm what is good is a habit of caring— to notice, remember, and acknowledge the positive around us.

Affirmation also tends to reduce negativity and defensiveness. A chronically critical attitude toward others often covers anxious and painful doubts about self. There is less need to be defensive when others are noticing and commenting on what you do well. Affirming strengths, efforts, good intentions, and common ground can also help to avert or resolve conflict (see chapter 15).

Try It!

Each day brings countless small opportunities to affirm, to notice and appreciate what others do. Affirming is like making small deposits into the bank of your relationships. More generally, affirmations express your attention to and compassion for the well-being of others. Choose a day to be particularly conscious of opportunities that you might otherwise miss to notice and affirm others' good qualities, efforts, actions, and strengths. Tomorrow would do. Experience and express your genuine appreciation for the good that is ever around us. You might even privately keep notes that day of what you affirmed. This is a particular kind of listening; being alert for the good that might otherwise have gone unnoticed.

Another way to hold onto what is good is to affirm someone whom you particularly admire or who has made a positive difference in your life. You could do this in conversation or in writing. It may be someone from the past whom you haven't seen for a while. Include specific examples of what you have appreciated.

Chapter 11

Expressing Yourself

When people don't express themselves, they die one piece at a time.

—Laurie Halse Anderson, *Speak*

Good listening can become too one-sided. If you practice high-quality reflective listening people will talk to you readily but may not listen much in return. In fact it's possible to hide behind good listening without revealing much about yourself, and others may happily go along with this. Close relationships, however, should involve two-way communication, with each partner having the opportunity to understand and be understood. This means not just listening but also expressing yourself, making yourself known. This chapter offers three simple ideas that can be useful in expressing yourself.

"I" Messages

One fundamental practice in communicating is the "I message," which can be particularly helpful in expressing feelings. It involves taking responsibility for your own reactions rather than blaming others. When feeling angry or hurt, for example, the immediate temptation is to begin with the accusing word "You":

- You only think about yourself.
- You hurt my feelings.
- You don't care about me.
- You're not listening to me!
- You are _____. (fill in the blank with a negative adjective)

In contrast, an I message usually begins with the word "I":

- I would like you to try to understand this from my perspective as well.
- I feel _____. (fill in the feeling: hurt, sad, happy, discouraged, lonely)
- I like it when you _____.

Note that there is an important difference between feelings and thoughts, although the two are related. The following statements are actually not about feelings:

- I feel that you are insensitive. (A very thinly disguised "You" statement)
- I feel it's important for us to make decisions like this together.

Here's a simple guideline: If the word "that" fits in logically after the word "feel," then it's not a feeling. More likely it's a thought, an opinion, or a belief (though there may be an unspoken feeling attached). Sometimes people use the word "feel" to signal a strong belief. "I feel our group should support this" can mean "I strongly believe that our group ought to support this, and you should believe that, too"; perhaps even, "You're wrong if you disagree with me." Though the word "that" might be unsaid, if it logically fits after the word "feel" then it's not a feeling. In this statement:

- "I feel (that) this is the right thing to do"

The unspoken word "that" is the tipoff that this is a thought or belief. On the other hand in a feeling statement like "I feel sad" it doesn't make any sense to insert the word "that":

- "I feel (that) sad."

Do you hear the difference? Both thoughts and feelings can be expressed well as I statements and both are important. It's just helpful not to mix them up, not to disguise a thought or belief as a feeling.

Again this is a contribution from Thomas Gordon, who further suggested how to use I statements to request a change. There are three parts to such an I statement: (1) your feeling, (2) the reason or context for the feeling, and (3) a specific request. For example:

- I feel lonely (1) when it seems like you aren't listening to me (2). Will you please make sure that you understand what I'm feeling before you respond (3)?

- I feel worried (1) when you leave your toys on the steps like this because someone might trip on them and be hurt (2). I want you to pick them up, please, and never leave toys on the stairs (3). OK?

- I feel frustrated (1) when I just want be heard and you start suggesting solutions (2). Sometimes all I want is for you to listen and understand (3).

Partial Responsibility and Offer to Help

It can also be helpful in relationships to communicate partial responsibility when appropriate and to offer to do your part. What might be your own piece of the puzzle?

- I feel anxious when it's getting time to leave and you don't seem to be ready. I know I'm too concerned sometimes about getting places early and I tend to hover. (Partial responsibility)

How can I do better in letting you know when I'd like to go? (Offer to help)

- I don't like it when it's getting time to go and you're bugging me about being ready. I know I don't pay as much attention to time as you do, and sometimes we're late for things. (Partial responsibility) If you can let me know when you would like to leave about an hour ahead of time (Specific request for change), I'll try to do better in being ready. (Offer to help)

Assertiveness

In most relationships there is a process of balancing needs. Whether those in relationship are individuals, groups, or nations, they choose how to assert their own needs. At one extreme is an aggressive approach that seeks to fulfill one's own needs at the expense of the other, implying that "My needs are more important than yours." Some words associated with this approach are coercing, bullying, dominating, forcing, and intimidating.

At the opposite extreme is a more passive approach that accedes to the other's needs and wishes at the expense of one's own. Some words associated with this approach are docile, submissive, acquiescent, subservient, and obedient. Of course self-sacrifice can be chosen voluntarily, even admirably in particular situations, but over time it is a troubled relationship that fulfills only one partner's needs.

In between these two extremes is the middle ground of assertiveness, an appropriate balancing that communicates respect and concern for others' needs as well your own.[12] It is the art of compromise and negotiation. Assertive people do not always insist on their own way, nor do they always sacrifice their own well-being. They refuse either to dominate or to be dominated. Here are a few examples of (1) aggressive, (2) passive, and (3) assertive options.

- The situation: Alex is invited to a social gathering with a free open bar. He would like to have a few drinks before going home. His wife is not going, and does not want him to drive with alcohol in his bloodstream. What to do?

1. Alex has several drinks and drives home, disregarding the potential harm to self and others of driving under the influence.

2. Alex foregoes the free drinks and drives home sober.

3. Alex has one drink, then waits an hour before driving so that his blood alcohol level will be at or near zero.

- Alex and Avery are going to a party together. More of an introvert, Avery wears down quickly at social occasions and doesn't want to stay long. Alex, however, enjoys socializing and likes to stay till the party's over.

  1. Avery wants to leave but Alex keeps the car keys and insists that they stay.

  2. Alex resentfully agrees to leave early and goes home grumbling at Avery.

  3. They take two cars to the party or otherwise arrange separate transportation.

A basic assumption behind assertiveness is that "Your needs and desires count, and so do mine." I count and you count. Rather than a win/lose struggle, an assertive approach seeks a way for both to win, for both parties' interests to be honored and met. Assertiveness (and not passivity) is also the essence of nonviolent resistance.[13]

Try It!

Think of a situation in which you have felt unhappy or frustrated with someone. It's easy to come up with blaming statements that begin with "You." How might you instead offer an "I" statement? "I feel _____(feeling) when you _____(specific behavior)." Remember that the word "that" does not belong after "feel." If a statement of partial responsibility might be appropriate, what could it be? Might you also include a specific, non-blaming request for change?

Or think of a real-life situation in which your own needs are balanced against and sometimes conflict with someone else's needs and preferences. It's easy to think of ways in which one person wins and the other loses out, though in such situations it is usually the relationship that really loses. What would be a possible outcome in which you both "win," both having at least part of what you would like?

Chapter 12

Listening Well in Relationships

Let there be spaces in your togetherness. And let the winds of the heavens dance between you. Love one another, but make not a bond of love: Let it rather be a moving sea between the shores of your souls. Fill each other's cup but drink not from one cup.

—Kahlil Gibran, *The Prophet*

Our lives are nourished by relationships that rely upon communication. Whether between individuals or groups, relationships necessarily involve differences. The partners vary in their assumptions, characteristics, and preferences; they bring to the relationship different strengths and abilities. At least in intimate relationships, differences can be the very chemistry of attraction, with each offering something that the other may long for or lack. Yet there is often then a temptation to try to remake the other in one's own image, and if that project were to succeed it would dismantle the original basis for attraction! Similarly, part of the charm of traveling is to encounter differences in geography, assumptions, architecture, and ways of life. If the visited place were "reformed" to duplicate one's familiar context, the charm would be gone.

Understanding and Valuing Differences

Each person or group brings some assumptions into a relationship. These may be unspoken or can be as formal as a written contract or mission statement. Why are we together? What is the purpose of our relationship? What are our hopes together and as individuals?

Chapter 4 described some attitudes of mind and heart that underlie empathic understanding. These same elements form a solid foundation for mutuality in relationship: a willingness to see with another's eyes, to suspend self-centeredness, to receive respectfully what the other has to offer, and to desire their well-being. Of course not all relationships are based on mutuality. Some are abusive and exploitive. Some simply occur by people having been thrown together in common circumstance or conflict. I write here about relationships that are consented to as mutual, with compassion for and commitment to each other's well-being. These need not be intimate bonds. In marketing, for example, there has been a shift in emphasis away from merely making sales toward developing ongoing customers who are satisfied that their needs have been well met. Such mutuality can emerge among friends, colleagues and coworkers, between nations, and within organizations and congregations.

One foundational supposition in mutuality is that there is value in understanding each other's experience and perspective. This requires a willingness to step outside of one's own limited frame of reference. Understanding others' perspectives is important in personal relationships, and its larger social value is also recognized in organizational movements like appreciative inquiry[14] and transformational leadership.[15]

A second supposition of mutuality is respect for and valuing of differences. Carl Jung described "psychological types," specific ways in which people differ from each other.[16] The most familiar of Jung's dimensions is introversion versus extraversion. Both are normal psychological types with differing characteristics. Four such dimensions were combined in the Myers-Briggs Type Indicator,[17] originally developed after World War II as a peacemaking tool. Unlike many psychological instruments, it is impossible to receive bad news from this one. The premise is that all types are equally valuable, with differing strengths and preferences, and that understanding these normal differences (rather than clashing over which personality type is right or best) is a key in communication and relationships.[18] Other systems such as the Enneagram[19] similarly describe differing and complementary psychological types.

A third aspect of mutuality is collaboration, working together in good will with common purpose. A relationship of mutuality is not one-sided but reciprocal, with each partner's needs honored. Listening well is a vital skill in all three aspects of mutuality: understanding another's perspective, appreciating differences, and collaborating.

How is Reflective Listening Different from Conversation?

In a conversation or discussion, people take turns offering their own perspectives. *Pure* reflective listening does none of that. Its sole purpose is to understand the other person's meaning and experience. As you are learning the skill of empathic listening, you will think of many things that you might ordinarily say or ask from your own experience, but the process here is to follow the *other* person's meaning and experience and reflect it back. As you do, you learn more than you would have if you had been asking questions or stating your own perspectives, and often much more quickly.

Once you have developed comfort and skill with reflective listening it can become part of ordinary conversations. You take time and listen well to make sure that you understand before jumping in with your own perspectives. Then, in normal conversation, you can alternate between reflective listening and self-expression. Ideally the other person also listens well to you, and you both take turns expressing and listening.

To gain skill and comfort with this particular way of listening, however, it is useful to practice only or primarily relying on reflection instead of asking questions. The "Try It!" exercise at the end of this chapter is one opportunity for such practice, but life offers many opportunities to practice even if the other person is unaware that you are doing so. It might be just for a minute or two, or it could be longer. You don't have to explain what you're doing; it may be better if you don't announce it and become self-conscious. Every time you offer a reflective listening statement you find out how accurate your reflection was and you learn more about what the person means. This is how you get better at forming reflections over time.

Resist the temptation to ask so many questions. Usually a question can be turned into a reflection. As suggested earlier, if you do ask a question, follow it up with at least two reflections as the person answers it. Also resist the temptation to practice any other roadblocks (chapter 5). See what happens when you rely on reflective listening. Whether or not they know it, the people you talk to become your teachers.

Try It!

Here is a way for two people to practice the skill of listening well. You each get a turn being the Speaker for about 7-10 minutes. When you are the Speaker, talk about something that *you feel two ways about* and haven't really made up your mind (or heart) about. You feel ambivalent, pulled in two different directions. Ambivalence is human nature, so it shouldn't be hard to find a topic. It could be most anything: a choice or decision, a job, a religious or social issue, a politician, a relationship, a request, a risk, where you live, how you spend your time, upsizing or downsizing, a donation, or a possible purchase.

It's the Listener who does the hard work. First, in order to set the topic, find out what the person feels two ways about, and then rely as much as you can on reflective listening. In the course of listening well you may ask up to *two* questions, and no more. Again, questions can often be turned into reflections. Don't use up your two questions by asking them in a row! When you do ask one of your two questions, follow it up with reflections. Also avoid leading questions like, "But don't you agree that . . . " This exercise is challenging, but it's a good way to discover how much it's possible to rely on reflective listening without having to ask questions. Keep out of the Speaker's ambivalence. Don't favor one side or the other, nor do you need to help the Speaker reach a conclusion or resolution. Your only goal is to listen and understand the ambivalence without judgment.

Here is a short sample of how such an exchange might go. The topic is an issue that has been passionately debated in politics within the U.S. and elsewhere. The Listener focuses on understanding both sides of the Speaker's dilemma without favoring either side or interjecting personal perspectives. This further illustrates how pure reflective listening is different from discussion or debate in which both people are expressing their views.

> Speaker: I guess something I feel two ways about is abortion. Mostly I come down on the pro-life side that all life is sacred.
>
> Listener: Human life.
>
> S: Not just people. I don't like shelters that kill homeless dogs and cats, or sacrificing laboratory animals. I mean, I'm not a vegetarian so I guess I'm not completely consistent there, but it seems like there is something sacred about life.
>
> L: And you said that's *mostly* what you think.
>
> S: Right. After all, who are we to say who lives and who dies? And at the same time when it comes right down to practical reality, who am I to make a woman's decision for her? If a woman is raped, it doesn't feel right to me to force her to have the baby. I'm not sure how you'd even do that.
>
> L: So in some ways you respect both life and choice.
>
> S: Crazy, isn't it? I mean, you're not supposed to sit on the fence about something as important as this. We're talking about life, when a fetus is a real human being.

L: What do you think about that? (First question; could have been a reflection instead)

S: Well, it seems pretty arbitrary to draw a line somewhere, like before this age it's not a life and then after that it is.

L: It doesn't seem that black and white to you.

S: No, it doesn't. In one way, there's at least the potential for life at the moment of conception.

L: You might even be opposed to contraception like the morning after pill.

S: I don't know! Again, who am I to be making decisions like that for another woman? And then I think, "Well, who's that woman to be making a decision about another life?" Murder is wrong, after all. I mean, I think even capital punishment is barbaric.

L: That's where it gets really confusing for you— when contraception or abortion is like murder.

S: Not confusing exactly. It's like I can see *both* sides of this, and that gets me in trouble.

L: When has that happened to you? (Second question; again it could have been a reflection)

S: Well, most of the people I know do have pretty strong opinions about this on one side or the other, and I don't like to get into discussions about it. One guy told me that I'm not a Christian unless I'm completely opposed to all abortion.

L: He seemed pretty sure about that.

S: It's like he was threatening me. "Unless you believe what I do, you're going to hell."

L: So you wonder about that, too.

S: No, not really. He's entitled to his opinion, like I am to mine.

L: If you just knew what it was.

S: Exactly!

Except for the two questions, all of the Listener's responses were reflections, usually continuing the paragraph. Even without being a part of this exchange there may have been points in the dialogue where you felt a strong inclination to insert your own beliefs, and in a two-sided discussion or debate you might do so. The challenge here, particularly on what can feel like a hot topic, is to suspend your own stuff for the time being and focus on listening in order to understand the person's dilemma. It's also good practice in sticking with empathic listening.

Now try it!

Chapter 13

Empathic Understanding in Close Relationships

> Most people see the problem of love primarily as that of
> *being loved,* rather than that of *loving.* Love is primarily
> giving, not receiving. Love is the active concern for the
> life and the growth of that which we love.
>
> —Erich Fromm, *The Art of Loving*

Listening well and, more generally, communicating well is one of the most important foundations for enduring friendship and intimate relationship. Empathic listening communicates interest in and caring for the other's life experience. The same skills described in prior chapters are all the more applicable in close relationships. It doesn't matter if both people are aware of using these particular skills. In fact it is a kindness to do so, and ideally you both do it for the other person, yourself, and your relationship. It is best when both (or all) people in a relationship understand what quality listening involves, learning and practicing together. Over time such listening can become second nature so that you're not even aware of "doing something." It becomes a way of being together.

Listening well is an investment in the quality of a relationship. Consider how empathic listening skills might contribute to healthy relationship between people who live together. Like anything else worth doing, listening well takes time. Some people intentionally set aside special time, like a date or an appointment, for the primary purpose of listening well to each other. Some have family conversations at the dinner table, turning off music or TV and silencing phones or other devices. For people who are most alert in the morning, it might be at the breakfast table, but this may not be the best time for evening people who function better at night. In any event, the more life becomes noisy and busy, the more important it is to have designated times for listening well.

Turn-taking is one simple approach. One person at a time takes a turn to talk, perhaps for a pre-agreed length of time. This does not mean that the other(s) must remain silent, although that is one option. As described earlier, reflective listening is an interactive process that can be practiced when someone is talking. The Listener(s) would refrain from roadblocks (chapter 5), with a primary goal of understanding the Speaker's experience. Reflective listening statements and occasional questions can help with this. Alternatively the Speaker might talk without interruption, followed by time for the Listener(s) to respond with what they understood of the person's experience, again avoiding roadblocks.

Here is an example of a Listener trying to practice accurate empathy while a Speaker talks. The Listener and Speaker happen to be brothers, sitting down together after a day at work.

> Listener: How was your day today? (Open question)
>
> Speaker: OK, I guess. The day just seemed to drag by.
>
> L: A pretty slow day. (Simple reflection)
>
> S: Not really. It was busy, but I was watching the clock and sometimes it seemed like the hands hardly moved.
>
> L: Like waiting for water to boil. (Analogy)
>
> S: Yes! I couldn't wait for the day to be over.
>
> L: You look excited— like there's something you were looking forward to. (Reflection)
>
> S: I've got a date tonight. Kind of a blind date, actually.

L: That can be exciting and also nerve-wracking. (Reflection)

S: I don't know anything about her. We met online, and you know how that is.

L: People don't always tell the truth, or the whole truth. (A guess, a reflection continuing the paragraph)

S: That's for sure. But I liked how she sounded.

L: Like someone you might be interested in. (Reflection)

S: Yeah, I think so. I guess I'll find out.

Except for the opening question and the first simple reflection, all of the Listener's responses here are complex reflections that make a guess about what his brother means and keep the conversation flowing. As reflecting becomes easier it flows like a smooth conversation. There were opportunities for roadblocks at every turn (like teasing, advice, warning, or changing the subject), but the Listener stuck with pure reflective listening.

Now here is another example with a couple mentioned in chapter 3, one of whom works in an office building while the other (Speaker) is mostly at home. Remember the situation: that the Speaker was hoping for some cozy time together after dinner, but sees the partner apparently getting ready to go back to work. Neither had communicated these plans to the other. In this case the Speaker asks to be listened to first:

Speaker: It looks like you're planning to go back to work, but before you do are you willing to take a few minutes to talk? I have something I want to say, and I'd like you to just hear me.

Listener: Uh oh! That doesn't sound good.

S: I just want to take a few minutes to tell you what I'm feeling while you listen quietly. Then I'd like you to tell me how you understand what I said. OK?

L: OK. So there'll be a test afterward. (Grins)

S: Just listen, please. I was really hoping that after dinner tonight we could just have some nice time together to talk, maybe make love later. I miss how we used to go for walks and just talk to each other. (I messages) Now, I realize I didn't let you know what I was feeling, and I should have told you when you got home. (Taking partial responsibility) I've been feeling pretty lonely lately here in the house, and I look forward all day to your getting home. I love it when we spend time together, and that's important to me. It doesn't have to be tonight, although that would be really nice, but if you do need to work are you willing for us to choose another night for just "us" time? (Specific request). Now before you respond, please just tell me what you understand about what I'm feeling.

L: Um, that you've been feeling lonely lately and you would really like me to stay home tonight and spend time with you?

S: Uh huh. Good. Anything else?

L: It doesn't have to be tonight, but if not, then you want us to set some time together soon. And I guess you're telling me that you love me. (Sheepish grin)

S: Yes! You got it!

Apart from what they decide, here's an example of listening first and then summarizing what was said before responding. The Listener's summaries were pretty good reflective listening statements (though the first one was turned into a question).

This same method can be used with turn-taking, talking about an agreed-upon topic. One partner speaks for a period of time while the other listens, then the Listener summarizes what she or he understood about the Speaker's meaning and experience. The Speaker adds anything important that the Listener left out, then they switch roles and the Listener becomes the Speaker. Remember that the Listener's response just reflects understanding, not agreement or disagreement, offense or defense. In other words, no roadblocks.

When trying this it's best not to start with difficult or "hot button" topics. Pick something interesting but not loaded. Another option long used in relationship enrichment groups is for both partners to write out their responses separately, then take turns reading their own words while the partner listens and afterward summarizes what she or he heard. Here are some examples of topics you might use in this way in listening to someone with whom you have a close relationship:

- Describe for me an experience from your life that you think might be difficult for me to understand.

- Tell me about a time when you experienced real joy, wonder, or awe.

- Who would you say was your best friend when you were growing up? What was this person like, and what made them your best friend?

- Tell me about someone you know or knew who you think grew old well.

- What would you say are three life experiences that had an important impact on the person you are today? What did you learn from each one?

- Who are three people who helped in an important way to shape the person you are today? What did each one do that was particularly important or meaningful to you?

- What would you say are the three most important values that guide your life now? What matters most to you?

Understanding or Problem Solving?

A common source of misunderstanding happens when one person is describing their experience, and instead of listening the other begins to offer solutions. Imagine a couple who live together with children. One partner arrives home from work to a barrage of frustration.

You won't believe the day I've had today! I had a whole list of things I was going to get done and then the school called and told me to come get Melanie, who was feeling sick. I picked her up and now she seems fine, but I've had to look after her all day, and besides that the phone kept ringing and interrupting me and I didn't get a thing done. The sink is still full of dishes, and I didn't even get the laundry done.

Is the person venting and just wanting to be heard, or would it be better to offer a problem-solving response like these:

Well, look, I'm pretty good at helping people to get better organized. It's part of what I do in my job. Why don't we look at your list and I can help you prioritize.

or

Well, I guess you could just turn off the phone.

or

Maybe next time you could sit in the nurse's office with Melanie for a few minutes, perhaps have the nurse take her temperature and see if she starts feeling better.

or even

OK, well, I'll get these dishes done while you start the laundry.

What do you think the frustrated partner might say next? Or would it be better to try some reflective listening and affirmation like:

Wow! What a frustrating day. You must be exhausted.

or

Sounds overwhelming! I'm sorry it's been such a hard day and I really appreciate how you take such good care of the kids.

or

> It's so hard to get anything done when there are constant interruptions like that. How do you manage it all?

On the other hand, reflective listening alone isn't very satisfying if the person really is looking for help and solutions. It's possible to ask which way you should go. Suppose a friend calls you and describes conflicts he is having with people in the apartment building where he lives. You might ask:

> Tell me how you'd like me to be your friend here. I'm happy to listen to you about what's happening and how it's affecting you. I'm also willing to help you think about different ways you might respond. Or maybe something else would be more helpful. What's the best way for me to be your friend right now?

If asking this doesn't feel right, a reasonably safe alternative is to start off with some reflective listening and see where it goes. Then you could invite the person's own ideas by asking something like, "What do you think you'll do?" If you offer any suggestions of your own, it's often a good idea to ask permission first. "Would it be all right if I mention some ideas that I've had, and you can tell me if any of these make sense to you?"

And of course the Speaker can also signal in advance what she or he would like. In the earlier example the stay-at-home partner began in exactly this way: "Are you willing to take a few minutes to talk? I have something I want to say, and I'd like you to just hear me."

Collaboration: A Mutual Responsibility

Empathy inspires compassion and action for the other's well-being. In relationship the mutual practice of empathic understanding nourishes a commitment to each other's health and happiness. But what makes your friend or partner happy? A natural inclination is to offer whatever makes *you* happy, but needs and preferences do differ, and often it's opposites that attract. Empathic listening can help two people understand what makes each other happy.

The Power of P's and D's

A direct approach that I have sometimes used when counseling couples is to have each person list their "P's and D's," their Pleases and Displeases. P's are things your partner does or can do that please you; they help you feel happy and loved. D's on the other hand, are things that displease you; you may feel hurt or unhappy when your partner does these. Just for your own reflection it's an interesting exercise to list these P's and D's. You can take it a step further and guess what your partner might list as P's and D's, the things you do that are pleasing or displeasing.

Unless you're careful to prevent it, there tends to be a natural drift in relationships over time. Early in an intimate relationship the P's are very powerful. A look, a kind word, a kiss, or a touch can be thrilling. As a relationship matures there is a natural decrease in the power of P's. A touch or a compliment is not as exciting as it once was. It's a natural process of getting used to each other. A compliment from an attractive stranger might be thrilling, whereas the same words from one's partner may have less impact. Because over time P's have less immediate influence, people tend to practice them less, which to a partner can feel like "being taken for granted."

The impact of D's in a loving relationship is just the opposite. A snub or criticism from a stranger can be easily dismissed and forgotten. To be sure, some people are exquisitely sensitive to any slight rejection, but rebuffs do tend to have less impact from someone with whom there is no history. There are also characteristically negative people who typically respond in a critical, judgmental, and disapproving manner. Over time people just tune them out, and their D's lose power to influence: "Don't take it personally. She's always like that." Within a loving relationship, however, D's can really sting. In Saint-Exupéry's classic story, a fox tells *The Little Prince*,[20] "You become responsible, forever, for what you have tamed." A criticism or rejection from someone you really care about can feel devastating. It's a contrast effect. Within a long history of P's, a D can be something of a shock. The opposite is also true. The rare compliment can be elating when it comes from a supervisor who is chronically hypercritical.

What this means is that we have a particular responsibility to mind our D's within caring relationships. For someone with whom you are generally positive and loving, an occasional zinger can really sting. Therein lies a danger in long-term relationships. As the P's naturally begin to have less influence over time, a D may get results (though not always the ones you want). Thus a loving relationship can drift toward aversive influence. That's the usual state of affairs by the time distressed couples come for counseling. They are mostly sniping at each other, and the P's have nearly vanished. Ironically, even the D's will lose their influence over time. This is not at all an irreparable situation. More importantly, it is preventable.

So what does all this have to do with listening? Remember that empathic listening is all about understanding the other person's inner experience. We do not automatically know what pleases someone else. We can make guesses, but as illustrated in chapter 3, such guesses are often wrong. Reflective listening is a process of checking your guesses until you get it right, and "right" here means understanding the other person's experience. Even with loving intention it's still possible to be giving someone what pleases you instead of what pleases them.

That's why I have encouraged distressed couples to begin minding their P's and D's. It starts with each person writing out their own lists, with encouragement to make the P list as long as possible. (Usually by the time people get into relationship counseling, the D list is already quite long enough.) Then they exchange lists to learn what their partner experiences as P's and D's. From there, each person's responsibility to their relationship is to increase their own P's while decreasing their D's. For a period of time both of them pay conscious attention to and keep count of their own P's and D's, as well as those they experience from their partner. Both are individually responsible to increase their own ratio of P's to D's, regardless of what the partner is doing. (Otherwise it can fall back into an endless cycle of retribution: "You displeased me, so I'm going to displease you.") Think of P's as deposits in the bank of your relationship, and each D as a withdrawal.

Of course you don't have to wait to be distressed before you start minding your P's and D's. Becoming more conscious of how your behavior affects each other and making positive changes can be valuable at any point in relationships, and is far easier before habits and hard feelings become entrenched. It can also be interesting for a while to keep track of the P's and D's you offer in the course of a day to people in general. Although you won't know everyone's list of their P's and D's, you can make pretty good guesses about how your words and actions are likely to be received.

Asking for Change

People in relationship also need a way to ask for change from each other. A good sequence for doing so is:

1. Be clear that you are making a request. For example: "I'd like to ask you to do something for me," or "I wonder if you'd be willing to try something different that I think will strengthen our relationship."

2. Make your request specific. A general request like "I want you to be nicer" isn't clear enough. You may know what you mean, but the other person probably doesn't. Focus on specific things that the person can do: "When we're talking, please look me in the eyes and don't be fiddling with your cell phone," or "Please check with me before you schedule something for both of us."

3. Ask the person to say in their own words what it is that you are requesting, to be sure they understand.

4. Ask whether the person is willing to do this.

5. Express your appreciation to the person for listening.

It can also be helpful to take partial responsibility as appropriate, or offer to help in some way with the desired change.

If you are receiving such a request, your role is to make sure that you understand. You might feel defensive, but first priority is to understand clearly what is being asked of you. Only then are you prepared to decide whether you are willing and able. "I'll try" implies that you are willing but you have your doubts about whether it's possible for you. A clearer commitment is "I will" or "I'll give it my best." I don't generally recommend offering a trade: "I'll do this for you if you will _____." Such deals can quickly unravel as soon as one person is imperfect, which of course we all are.[21] Like listening well, change is about persistence.

Keeping a loving relationship healthy and strong is a long-distance journey. The earlier you begin to practice empathic listening and being mindful of your Ps and Ds, the better.[22] Life brings natural waves of joy and woe, and each passes.[23] Stay with it. When relationships become more distressed there is a common pattern whereby one partner makes more urgent demands while the other increasingly withdraws.[24] It is a relationship death spiral, but not irreversible if changed in time. When working with distressed couples I found it particularly important to promptly interrupt their over-practiced patterns of zinging each other and help them begin taking positive steps toward healing their relationship. Quick fixes are rare and sometimes repair takes quite a while. Better still to begin practicing empathic understanding early, and accept responsibility to contribute to each other's happiness and well-being.

Try It!

Think of a significant relationship in your own life. If you were to construct lists of your P's and D's— the things that the other person does that particularly please and displease you— what would be on your lists? Is one list longer than the other? Now imagine what the other person might say if they were writing down their own P's and D's from you. Remember that this is your imagination— the things you come up with may be very different from what the other person would actually say. What might happen if you both wrote down your P's and D's lists and exchanged them?

If you were to ask for one specific change from a person you care about, how exactly might you word your request using the guidelines in this chapter?

Practice the skills of empathic understanding with a significant person in your life. Ideally it would be someone who is also working on learning the skills described in this book. Again, don't start with a tense or difficult subject, but choose one of the topics offered earlier in this chapter. If you're introducing this exercise to someone who's not familiar with what you're doing, you might explain it something like this (but in your own words):

> I'm trying to learn how to listen better, and I wonder if you'd be willing to help me practice. You could choose a topic from this list—something you could talk about for maybe five minutes, and I'll do my best to listen well. Along the way I'll be checking to make sure that I'm understanding well. Then whenever you've finished I'll give you a short summary of what I heard, and you can tell me how I did.

If the other person is also practicing these skills, you could then switch roles while you talk as Speaker about one of the topics for five minutes or so.

Chapter 14

Listening for Values

There is no happiness if the things we believe in are different than the things we do.

—Albert Camus

As listening well becomes easier over time, and as you get to know people better you may begin to understand the values that underlie their immediate thoughts and actions. Conscious of it or not, we each have a system of values that guide how we perceive and behave in the world. We can help each other become more conscious of what we care most about, so that we may intentionally live with greater integrity to our core values.[25]

Listening for values goes beyond the superficial. The values to which we aspire may not come up in daily small talk. This form of listening goes below the surface to explore (with permission) the guiding goals or intentions behind behavior.

If you want to go deeper, to listen for values underlying a person's current experience, it is again tempting to ask analyzing questions:

- Why do you believe that?

- What are you hoping to accomplish?

- What makes you do that?

It's not wrong to ask such questions, but as discussed in chapter 8, questions place at least an unconscious pressure to answer. Questions may appeal to your curiosity, but I find it is usually better to rely on reflecting what you hear, as well as what has not quite been said but might be meant. Here's an example:

> Speaker: I'm just not comfortable with what my supervisor is asking me to do, to keep certain things off the books.
>
> Listener: It doesn't seem right to you.
>
> S: I don't believe it is. I do want to keep my job, and I think I understand what he's trying to do, but this could get me in trouble.
>
> L: Like legal trouble.
>
> S: Or within the company even. I don't know if his boss even knows about this.
>
> L: What bothers you most about this is that it could get you in trouble down the line.
>
> S: Well, if I do what he wants, I don't know where it would go next.
>
> L: Once you open that door . . .
>
> S: Yeah. But mostly it's just not right.
>
> L: Sounds kind of like lying.
>
> S: Well, it would be. I guess that's what really bothers me. I wasn't raised to be dishonest.
>
> L: So it's not just that you could get in trouble. It goes against what believe, what you learned in growing up.
>
> S: Right. What is that old saying about a tangled web once you start deceiving? It just gets more and more complicated.
>
> L: It's just easier to be honest.
>
> S: And there's less to remember. (Smiles)

All of the Listener's responses are reflective listening statements. They might have arrived at the same place if the Listener had asked questions like, "What are you worried about?" Yet that focuses the Listener's attention on *worries* like getting caught, and worry is not the whole picture. Even well-intentioned questions can narrow the conversation. In this case, the Speaker came around to what seems to be an underlying value of honesty.

It also happens that values we hold can come into conflict with each other. In chapter 12 there was a practice exercise in which the Speaker talked about "something that you feel two ways about," and the Listener's task was to listen well in order to understand both sides of the dilemma. The "two ways" often have to do with at least two closely held values that in this particular situation come into conflict with each other.

- I love my child *and* also disapprove of what she is doing.

- I believe this is the right thing for people to do, *and* I also believe that people should be free to make their own decisions.

- Part of me wants to help, *and* part of me is just tired of helping.

In circumstances like this, *both* values matter and the struggle is how to reconcile or choose between them. Such ambivalence is one situation where it can be particularly helpful to talk it over with someone who knows how to listen well without caving in to the urge to fix it, take sides, or give advice.[26]

About Ambivalence

Ambivalence is a conflict within, often the clashing of two or more values. There are five things that it's helpful to know about ambivalence.

1. The first is that it's absolutely normal. You want something and at the same time you also don't want it. Part of you prefers this, and another part isn't so sure. You care about X and you also care about Y and Z, all at the same time. You're not crazy. That's human nature.

2. Ambivalence is a place where you can get stuck for a long time. When you're considering making some change, for example, a common pattern is to think of a reason why you might do it, then think of a reason not to, and then stop thinking about it because ambivalence is uncomfortable. It seems easier not to think about it.

3. Ambivalence comes in three flavors. The easiest kind— a *Go/Go* conflict— is being torn between two (or more) positive possibilities, both of which you want but which are incompatible. It's the candy store problem. Then there's the *Stop/Stop* conflict," being caught between "the devil and the deep blue sea" or "a rock and a hard place." This involves two (or more) possibilities, both of which you would like to avoid. The third is a *Stop/Go* conflict, where you both want and don't want something simultaneously; or worse, are torn between two things, both of which you want and don't want at the same time. That one can really make you crazy.

4. When you feel ambivalent and somebody tells you what you should do, a natural response is to argue for the opposite, and in the process you can literally talk yourself into going one particular way. Even if you agree with the person's arguments, the natural tendency is to move in the other direction. They may think they are doing you a favor, but someone who keeps arguing for one choice is likely to push you in the opposite direction.

5. The challenge in getting out of a jam like this is to resist the temptation to avoid thinking about it. One method for making up your mind about ambivalence was described in 1772 by Benjamin Franklin[27] and it probably goes back much farther than that. When considering two different possibilities, put a line down the middle of a sheet of paper. On one side (for Choice A) list the good things about making Choice A (which might also include disadvantages of Choice B). Then do the same for Choice B on the other side of the page: what would be the advantages of Choice B? Or you could fill in

four lists: the good things about Choice A, the less good things about Choice A, the good things about Choice B, and the less good things about Choice B. Making lists like this might help you realize it's a lot clearer than you thought. In any case, it helps you see the whole picture at once.[28]

How can a good listener be most helpful in this situation? Someone who knows how to listen patiently can certainly help an ambivalent person stay with the process long enough to get to a big picture. As a listener you might feel a desire to help the person decide; you may even want to push in a particular direction, but remember that doing so can have an unintended opposite effect. And for goodness' sake don't try some cute "reverse psychology" tactic. I think that the most friendly thing you can do is to listen well to both (or all) sides of the dilemma without trying to fix it.

What Do You Care Most About?

As is often the case, perhaps the best preparation for helping someone else clarify their values is first to become clearer about your own. At the end of this chapter is a long list that briefly describes various possible values, things that different people might hold dear. You may care about many of these to some extent. This is merely a list of a hundred possibilities that I have developed over the years with three colleagues.[29] There might well be other things that you value that are not on this list, and it's fine to add them. We developed it originally as a "card sort," with each value printed by itself on a small card.[30] The cards were then sorted into five piles: (1) Not important to me; (2) Somewhat important to me; (3) Important to me; (4) Very important to me; and (5) Most important to me. A simpler approach, though, is just to scan through the list and pick out no more than ten that you would identify as the most important guiding values in your life. Then if you want to take it a step further, see if you can arrange them in order of priority. What is truly *most* important to you as a guiding value for your life?

This can also be the basis for an interesting conversation with people you care about. What would they identify as their most important values? Even with people you've known for a long time, the result may surprise you (and them as well)! Instead of just making a list, find out more about how and why each is an important value. This can begin with an open question that you then, as usual, follow with reflective listening. Once a few "most important" values have been identified, here are some possible open questions to begin the discussion:

- In what ways is this an important value for you?

- Give me some examples of how you express this value in your life.

- Why do you think this is so important to you?

- When has it been most challenging for you to practice this value?

But don't rely too much on such questions; they are just starters. The point is to listen well as the person becomes clearer about what matters most. Ask an open question and then get out of the way with reflective listening:

> Listener: You picked out "challenge" as one of your key values. In what ways is this important to you?
>
> Speaker: I like to push myself, I guess.
>
> L: To find out what you can do.
>
> S: Or not just settle for what I already know how to do. I like to keep on growing.
>
> L: You're not satisfied with what you already know.
>
> S: No, I'm not! I mean, I've learned a lot, but am I just going to stop learning now?
>
> L: There are so many more possibilities.
>
> S: Way more! I get bored pretty quickly if I just keep doing the same things.

L: So some of it is keeping life interesting; curiosity, maybe.

S: I used to like the *Star Trek* movies when I was a kid. "Let's see what's out there!"

L: You don't like to settle for the way things are now.

S: Well, sometimes I guess that's a curse as well as a blessing. I'm kind of a restless person.

L: Another side of this "challenge" value is never quite feeling at home where you are.

S: Can't there be some kind of balance between the two?

L: Maybe there can.

S: I guess maybe that's what I'm looking for. But I don't want to lose that edgy feeling.

L: You kind of like the restlessness, and also you could probably enjoy the present a little more.

This last reflective statement is double-sided, reflecting both sides. This kind of double-sided reflection can be particularly helpful when someone is ambivalent. It reflects both themes that are emerging, with an "and" in the middle. Both things are true. When people are ambivalent, "Yes, but" is where they can get stuck. Isn't it interesting that the word "but" works something like an eraser? It diminishes the value of what went before. "You're a nice person and all, and I really like you, but . . . " Suddenly the preceding words fade away and you brace yourself for what's to come. An "and" values both what precedes it and what follows it. "You're a good person and I really enjoy hearing from you, and when you send me so many messages I have a hard time paying attention to them all."

The dialogue above is also a good example of "continuing the paragraph" as a way of empathic listening. With minor changes, all of the reflections could flow smoothly as the Speaker's own thought process, an internal monologue:

Speaker: I like to push myself, I guess, to find out what I can do and not just settle for what I already know how to do. I like to keep on growing. I'm not satisfied with what I already know. I mean, I've learned a lot, but am I just going to stop learning now? There are so many more possibilities. Way more! I get bored pretty quickly if I just keep doing the same things. So some of it is keeping life interesting; curiosity, maybe. I used to like the *Star Trek* movies when I was a kid: "Let's see what's out there!" I don't like to settle for the way things are now. Sometimes I guess that's a curse as well as a blessing. I'm kind of a restless person, and another side of this "challenge" value is never quite feeling at home where I am. Can't there be some kind of balance between the two? Maybe there can. I guess maybe that's what I'm looking for. But I don't want to lose that edgy feeling. I kind of like the restlessness, and also I could probably enjoy the present a little more.

In a way, the Speaker and Listener are telling a story together, the Listener's own story.

Try It!

From the list of possibilities that follows, what would you identify as a short list of the most important guiding values of your own life? No more than ten, and fewer is fine. Can you distinguish among them which one(s) you might place at the top, perhaps even more important than the rest on your list? How might you rank-order them? (It's fine if that step doesn't appeal to you.)

Here are some possible questions you could reflect on with each item on your short list:

- How do you suppose this came to be a core value for you? Were there important people who taught you this or modeled it for you?

- In what ways are you expressing this value in your life now? What are some good examples of how you put this value into practice?

- When has it been particularly difficult for you to practice this value? Was there some other value of yours that was conflicting with it?

- How might you express and practice this value more fully in your life? What opportunities are there?

With whom might you have a conversation about core values? Is there a particular friend or group with whom this could be an interesting relationship-building exercise? Take turns interviewing each other about the core values that you have identified, starting with open questions like those described in this chapter and following up with reflective listening.

Chances are you will have opportunities to listen well to someone on a topic about which they are ambivalent. It's very common. Can you imagine how this might go if you practiced the approach described in this chapter, rather than just keeping quiet or offering advice or other roadblocks? The next time this happens, give it a try.

One Hundred Possible Personal Values

1. ACCEPTANCE—to be accepted as I am

2. ACCURACY—to be correct in my opinions and beliefs

3. ACHIEVEMENT—to have important accomplishments

4. ADVENTURE—to have new and exciting experiences

5. ART—to appreciate or express myself in art

6. ATTRACTIVENESS—to be physically attractive

7. AUTHORITY—to be in charge of others

8. AUTONOMY—to be self-determined and independent

9. BEAUTY—to appreciate beauty around me

10. BELONGING—to have a sense of belonging, being part of

11. CARING—to take care of others

12. CHALLENGE—to take on difficult tasks and problems

13. COMFORT—to have a pleasant and comfortable life

14. COMMITMENT—to make enduring, meaningful commitments

15. COMPASSION—to feel and act on concern for others

16. COMPLEXITY—to embrace the intricacies of life

17. COMPROMISE—to be willing to give and take in reaching agreements

18. CONTRIBUTION—to make a lasting contribution in the world

19. COOPERATION—to work collaboratively with others

20. COURAGE—to be brave and strong in the face of adversity

21. COURTESY—to be considerate and polite toward others

22. CREATIVITY—to create new things or ideas

23. CURIOSITY—to seek out, experience, and learn new things

24. DEPENDABILITY—to be reliable and trustworthy

25. DILIGENCE—to be thorough and conscientious in whatever I do

26. DUTY—to carry out my duties and obligations

27. ECOLOGY—to live in harmony with the environment

28. EXCITEMENT—to have a life full of thrills and stimulation

29. FAITHFULNESS—to be loyal and true in relationships

30. FAME—to be known and recognized

31. FAMILY—to have a happy, loving family

32. FITNESS—to be physically fit and strong

33. FLEXIBILITY—to adjust to new circumstances easily

34. FORGIVENESS—to be forgiving of others

35. FREEDOM—to be free from undue restrictions and limitations

36. FRIENDSHIP—to have close, supportive friends

37. FUN—to play and have fun

38. GENEROSITY—to give what I have to others

39. GENUINENESS—to act in a manner that is true to who I am

40. GOD'S WILL—to seek and obey the will of God

41. GRATITUDE—to be thankful and appreciative

42. GROWTH—to keep changing and growing

43. HEALTH—to be physically well and healthy

44. HONESTY—to be honest and truthful

45. HOPE—to maintain a positive and optimistic outlook

46. HUMILITY—to be modest and unassuming

47. HUMOR—to see the humorous side of myself and the world

48. IMAGINATION—to have dreams and see possibilities

49. INDEPENDENCE—to be free from depending on others

50. INDUSTRY—to work hard and well at my life tasks

51. INNER PEACE—to experience personal peace

52. INTEGRITY to live my daily life in a way that is consistent with my values

53. INTELLIGENCE—to keep my mind sharp and active

54. INTIMACY—to share my innermost experiences with others

55. JUSTICE—to promote fair and equal treatment for all

56. KNOWLEDGE—to learn and contribute valuable knowledge

57. LEADERSHIP—to inspire and guide others

58. LEISURE—to take time to relax and enjoy

59. LOVED—to be loved by those close to me

60. LOVING—to give love to others

61. MASTERY—to be competent in my everyday activities

62. MINDFULNESS—to live conscious and mindful of the present moment

63. MODERATION—to avoid excesses and find a middle ground

64. MONOGAMY—to have one close, loving relationship

65. MUSIC—to enjoy or express myself in music

66. NON-CONFORMITY—to question and challenge authority and norms

67. NOVELTY—to have a life full of change and variety

68. NURTURANCE—to encourage and support others

69. OPENNESS—to be open to new experiences, ideas, and options

70. ORDER—to have a life that is well-ordered and organized

71. PASSION—to have deep feelings about ideas, activities, or people

72. PATRIOTISM—to love, serve, and protect my country

73. PLEASURE—to feel good

74. POPULARITY—to be well-liked by many people

75. POWER—to have control over others

76. PRACTICALITY—to focus on what is practical, prudent, and sensible

77. PROTECT—to protect and keep safe those I love

78. PROVIDE—to provide for and take care of my family

79. PURPOSE—to have meaning and direction in my life

80. RATIONALITY—to be guided by reason, logic, and evidence

81. REALISM—to see and act realistically and practically

82. RESPONSIBILITY—to make and carry out responsible decisions

83. RISK—to take risks and chances

84. ROMANCE—to have intense, exciting love in my life

85. SAFETY—to be safe and secure

86. SELF-ACCEPTANCE—to accept myself as I am

87. SELF-CONTROL—to be disciplined in my own actions

88. SELF-ESTEEM—to feel good about myself

89. SELF-KNOWLEDGE—to have a deep and honest understanding of myself

90. SERVICE—to be helpful and of service to others

91. SEXUALITY—to have an active and satisfying sex life

92. SIMPLICITY—to live life simply, with minimal needs

93. SOLITUDE—to have time and space where I can be apart from others

94. SPIRITUALITY—to grow and mature spiritually

95. STABILITY—to have a life that stays fairly consistent

96. TOLERANCE—to accept and respect those who differ from me

97. TRADITION—to follow respected patterns of the past

98. VIRTUE—to live a morally pure and excellent life

99. WEALTH—to have plenty of money

100. WORLD PEACE—to work to promote peace in the world

Chapter 15

Listening Well in Conflict

Education is the ability to listen to almost anything without losing your temper or your self-confidence.

—Robert Frost

A peculiar thing often happens in conflict situations: people just stop listening to each other. Once someone is identified as being on an "other" side, it's as if there is no point in listening to them, at least not on sensitive topics. It can happen in families and among friends, and can paralyze meetings or legislative and governing bodies.

Perhaps there is no situation in which listening well is more challenging than in the midst of conflict. Empathic listening may not be sufficient to resolve conflict, but at least it is a good start. The goal is first to understand a differing perspective. Good listening does not imply agreement. One might worry that "if I don't speak up and contest what I'm hearing, then I am accepting it." Not so. Understanding is only a beginning.

As a refresher, listening well in order to understand is quite different from the pattern of conversation in which you remain quiet just long enough to know how to disagree or to fit in your own perspective. For the time being you let go of making points or being clever. You let go of judging, labeling, and assuming that you already know. The one and only purpose of this kind of listening is to understand what matters most to someone, how they think and feel. The basic mental set for this kind of listening is *curiosity*—an interest and desire to know. This kind of listening requires at least three challenging disciplines.

1. Focusing to give your full undivided curious attention to understanding the person's own experience (chapter 6)

2. Refraining from roadblocks (chapter 5)

3. Empathic listening in which you try, like a good mirror, to reflect back what you think the person means as accurately as you can (chapter 8).

Empathic listening can be useful in understanding *any* kind of experience, but in this chapter we turn to three more demanding applications related to conflict. The first involves listening well to people with whom you disagree. Secondly, reflective listening can be useful in de-escalating anger and discord. Finally, accurate empathy can be a valuable component in conflict resolution.

Listening Across Canyons

Something in us longs to perceive the world as divided in two: us and them, black and white, east and west, right and wrong. It's simple. It's as though there are only two views, and the one that we ourselves hold just happens to be the correct one. It is an illusion, of course. There are as many different views as there are people. Politics and religion are often contentious and polarizing topics, but a dualistic way of perceiving reality can happen in many contexts including social groups (who's in and out), stereotyping, academic disciplines, and divorce courts. Binary thinking inspires conflict and division, which in turn are exacerbated when we stop listening to each other.

I believe it is valuable to listen well to people with whom we may disagree. It is, first of all, a broadening experience to understand perspectives that vary from one's own, and to break the habit of immediately dismissing differences without curiosity. Listening well may reveal unexpected commonalities that support collaboration and relationship. It also averts proceeding on mistaken assumptions. If our guesses can go so wrong about what a single statement means (chapter 3), how much more we can be mistaken when we make assumptions about someone's complex values and beliefs!

It's easier to practice this first with people with whom you're not in conflict, and whose views or values differ from your own. In truth this might be almost anyone, as long as you feel no ill will toward them, because anyone you choose will have perspectives at least somewhat different from yours, but do try to get outside your familiar comfort zone. Choose someone, for example, whose political or religious values are likely to be quite different from your own; the bigger the difference, the better. This is not a conversation, dialogue, discussion, or debate. It is an opportunity to practice listening well.

For most people it is quite an unusual experience to have someone listen well with no purpose other than to understand their perspective, particularly on a contentious topic. After all, in the course of a typical week, how many minutes of high-quality listening do you receive? For this reason it can be important to clarify in advance what you intend to do. When I wanted to get some practice in listening to people with political views very different from mine, I offered an invitation like this:

> It seems like people have stopped listening to each other when they have very different political opinions. We might talk *at* each other for a little while, but not really listen with interest and respect. I believe this is something we ought to be doing more, and I need practice! What I would like to do, if you're willing, is to interview you for an hour or so, with no purpose other than to understand better your own perspectives. My intention is to listen to you without interrupting, agreeing, or disagreeing, just to understand your own political values and what matters to you. I may ask a few questions but mostly I'll do my best to listen well. I'll tell you what I understood, and

then you can tell me how I did. Are you willing to help
me practice?

Yes, an hour. It's an unusual and inviting opportunity to be listened
to for a whole hour with no purpose other than understanding.
No one ever turned me down. Happily this is also the truth: we
do need practice at this! It is particularly challenging to listen well
on topics about which we may passionately disagree, suspending
at least for the time being the championing of our own views and
opinions. The word "interview" seems fitting here, because a good
interviewer seeks to understand and clarify. It's not an ordinary
conversation. The interviewer has a different role from that of the
person being interviewed. To be sure, some "interviewers" seem
mostly interested in promoting their own perspectives, but in my
opinion that is not good interviewing. Questions like, "Isn't it true
that _____?" or "Don't you agree that _____?" are loaded and
leading. They are more about argument than curiosity.

Instead, interview someone just to understand their beliefs.
Your own views are at least temporarily irrelevant to this process.
In fact, if you interview well, the Speaker may have very little idea
about what you personally believe. There is no intent to challenge
or change the Speaker's views— only to understand them

When listening across canyons—potentially divisive issues—
roadblocks can be over-practiced and almost automatic responses.
In a polarized context there is a temptation to reflexively dismiss a
differing viewpoint. Stay with the empathic listening process!

I have noticed that when speaking about a hot topic, people
often begin by revisiting some specific grievances about incidents
or people. If you listen well to these without putting up roadblocks,
it becomes possible to move past specifics toward more general
values and beliefs. Listen carefully and dive deeper. What do these
instances suggest that the Speaker's underlying ideals or principles
may be? Reflect those, knowing that you are making a guess. What
is "the Good" toward which the Speaker hopes to move? What are
the positive values that seem to guide the person's views? Politics,
for example, involves a balancing of complex competing interests, prioritizing among potentially conflicting values. What are

the values that, in this person's view, should have most priority? Beware relying too heavily on questions, and as usual follow any question with reflective listening. I find that many people have not considered in depth the foundations of their own beliefs. Specific and even strongly endorsed political views may not be clearly linked to underlying values. To be listened to well can bring a deeper understanding of one's own beliefs and the integrity among them.

There are likely to be some issues that are just too close to home for you to listen well. For whatever reason, there may be topics on which it is just too difficult to listen without judgment. Perhaps they touch on painful personal history, relate to unresolved conflicts, or disturb strongly-held values. Psychotherapists often discover that they are not well suited to work with particular types of clients or problems. This is normal. Listen well, and also recognize your own limits.

Listening in Tight Places

Empathic listening has long been used to "talk down" people who are quite agitated or angry. There is something calming about having a person listen to you well, understanding your experience, and it also helps to prevent miscommunication. These can be particularly useful skills in situations like education or community policing, where one person has a responsibility to keep calm, absorb negative energy without responding in kind, and calmly seek a resolution. Customer service is one such context, where "the customer is always right" even when they're not. Commonly advocated responses include reflective listening, apology, and accepting partial responsibility. Parenting is another situation in which the adult has a particular role and responsibility. Responding defensively or offensively in such situations is only likely to increase conflict and anger.

The following real life example, though, is between two peers on a phone call. It begins with an outraged Speaker.

Listener: Hello?

Speaker: Who do you think you are, telling my wife that I should take care of our kids? Our home life is none of your damned business!

L: It sounds like you're really upset with me. (Reflection)

S: You bet I am! What do you mean telling her that I should babysit while she goes out?

L: It seems like a real intrusion into your personal affairs. (Reflection)

S: Well, isn't it?

L: Tell me why this makes you so angry. (Question)

S: We both get home from work and she says she wants to go out on Thursday night and that you told her I should stay with the kids.

L: I can see how that would sound pushy of me! (Reflection)

S: Damn right. What were you thinking?

L: Honestly, I need to get six of us together, and Thursday night is OK for the other five so I was checking whether Carol could come, too. (Giving information)

S: And what does that have to do with me?

L: She said she had to be with the children, and I wondered whether it might be possible for you to mind them for a while. I guess that's where you think I stepped over a line. (Reflection)

S: You sure did.

L: So it sounded to you like I was trying to run your life or boss you around. (Reflection) I'm sorry that I offended you. That certainly wasn't my intention.

S: How we arrange our child care is between the two of us, period.

L: I accept that, and I apologize.

S: Apology accepted.

It's tempting to go on the defensive in a situation like this. "I don't think there's anything wrong with what I said. Can't you take care of the kids sometimes, too?" You can imagine the result. Sticking with empathic listening usually gets a much better response, and often calms things down quickly.

Of course there are times when you do need to establish limits or honor rules. In customer service there are certain restrictions on how accommodating you can or should be. This also happens in parenting, where consistency has its benefits. One way of being consistent is to acknowledge what the other person is saying while calmly repeating the limit or rule. In the era of vinyl records this was called the "broken record" technique, referring to a defect on the disk that would cause it to skip, repeating the same sounds over and over. Here's a fourteen-year-old Speaker and a parent:

Speaker: I'm going outside for a while. I'll finish up my homework when I get back.

Listener: No, sorry, the rule is that you get your homework done first.

S: But I don't have that much to do! It won't take much time at all.

L: I'm glad you don't have much left to do, and the rule is that you get your homework done first.

S: No way! My friends are waiting for me.

L: I know you're eager to see them, and your homework gets done first.

S: That's a stupid rule.

L: I appreciate that it's inconvenient for you right now, and yes, it's our rule: homework first.

S: But they'll be gone by the time I'm done!

L: That would be really disappointing for you. Homework first.

S: What am I supposed to tell them?

L: That we have a rule that you get your homework done first. Sorry! Call them and see if they would be willing to stick around until you finish that little bit of homework.

Beyond Listening Well

Listening well is valuable by itself, and can also provide a foundation for going further. In the "listening across canyons" example, you listen well to a friend's views on a controversial topic (and perhaps your partner also listens to you), which can be a basis for continuing dialogue that is not about winning or losing. It might be possible to discover some shared goals or beliefs that could form a basis for subsequent collaboration. Listening well is just a first step. Similarly, in "listening in tight places" you give priority to reflecting the other person's experience to make it clear that you "get" it. From there, it may be possible to negotiate a solution.

The same is true in resolving conflicts. Empathic listening is a good beginning to understand each other's perspectives and goals. A process of mediation often begins with mutual listening. In the presence of a mediator, each gets a chance to tell their story while the other listens, ideally without interrupting or raising roadblocks. When people are listened to well, they are often more willing to listen themselves. What do the two parties have in common? Perhaps both are unhappy with the status quo and would like to find a solution to make things better. What is each person willing to do, and what would each like the other to do? Mutual affirmation (chapter 10) can further diminish defensiveness and open up communication. Again, it is not about one winning and the other losing; mediation is about finding a mutually agreeable way forward that honors each person's needs and desires, at least in part. There are some clear similarities to healing in relationships (chapter 13).

Try It!

Listening Across Canyons

Start with someone you know, like, and/or respect, and also whose perspectives are likely to be quite different from your own. The differences of opinion might be in contentious areas such as politics, parenting, religion, or values. You can offer a one-way listening process, or propose that you both take listening time to understand each other's views. As indicated earlier, such an interview usually needs some explaining, such as: "I wonder whether you would be willing to take an hour to tell me over coffee what you think and feel about _____. Rather than this being a discussion or debate, I would like to interview you with no goal other than for me to better understand your own perspective and what matters to you. I won't be stating my own views, just listening to understand yours. I may ask you a few questions but mostly I'll do my best to listen well."

If you take time to listen to and understand another's perspective, it does not obligate that person to return the favor. If you will each do a listening session, however, it is not essential that the other person have experience with the specific skills described in previous chapters. If you are the first Listener, you set an example. The essential ground rule is to listen well with a goal of understanding, without discussion or debate. An hour is a good length of time for such a listening session. It is easiest to ask questions and then keep quiet, but here is an ideal opportunity to practice reflective listening.

Nevertheless, interviewers do often think in advance about questions they would like to ask. For example, here are some possible questions that might be asked in an interview to explore political values:

1. To what extent do you think we are responsible for each other's welfare in our society?

2. In what ways does your own spiritual or religious faith inform and guide your political beliefs?

3. From what, if anything, do you believe our government should protect us?

4. What are some things that you believe government should *not* do?

5. In thinking about the role of government, how do you personally balance the sometimes conflicting values of individual freedom and the common good?

6. When you think about the political issues about which you are most passionate, what does that indicate about your underlying values?

7. What do you believe about paying taxes and how tax funds should be used?

8. What kinds of decisions do you think are best made at different levels of government?

9. What is an issue on which you differ from the usual position of people who share many of your political views? How is your view different, and why?

These are only examples that explore more general underlying values. The interview process may suggest some different questions that you did not think of in advance. In any event, ask one open question at a time and then follow up with reflective listening.

Here is another challenge that focuses more specifically on a particular issue and so might require less time. Think of someone with whom you have a significant difference of perspective on this issue. Invite that person to have a conversation with you about this topic. Explain in advance that you do not want to argue or debate; instead you want simply to listen with a goal of understanding as best you can his or her perspective on the issue. Indeed, resist the temptation to disagree or try to persuade. Ask a few open questions, but mostly practice reflective listening to make sure you understand and to show that you do. At the end of the conversation offer the best summary you can of the person's perspective on this issue as you understand it, again without commentary or disagreement, and close by thanking her or him for the conversation. When you do this, you have already contributed to better understanding. If the person wants to return the favor, so much the better.

Listening in Tight Places

The next time someone seems angry at or hurt by you, try stepping into empathic listening to communicate that you understand. You do not necessarily have to accept partial responsibility, though in truth we do share fault more often than we might wish to recognize. Just listening well is a very positive step. Can you honestly acknowledge partial responsibility? Is an apology in order? Might some change decrease hurt feelings in the future? What would each of you like?

Beyond Listening Well

The next time you find yourself in a conflict, start by practicing empathic listening to make sure that you understand the other's perspective. Try restating their perspective in your own nonjudgmental terms, and ask whether you got it right. Mind the music in your voice and not just the words! Then ask the other to listen to your own perspective and tell you what they heard. What can you affirm in the other? What do you have in common? What would you like to have happen? What are you willing to do? What resolutions might be possible that would honor you both?

Chapter 16

The Promise of Empathic Understanding

It appears that religions—and perhaps even humanity itself—will not survive if we stay within tribal consciousness, believing our religion is the only "one true religion."

—Richard Rohr

Viewed in one way, empathic listening is a choice that you make, a skill that can be useful in certain situations when relating to others. It is an ability to be used now and then, that can make a positive difference.

Yet there is something about empathic understanding that grows on you. Opening the door to others' inner worlds is like discovering a library of fascinating stories you have never heard before and are eager to read. There is such a richness in experiencing the world through others' eyes as well as your own. As this awareness dawns, the quest for accurate empathy can become an everyday pursuit.

The magnetism of empathic understanding goes well beyond curiosity, however. Accurate empathy has a way of deepening relationships, diving beneath the superficiality of ordinary small talk. Conversations now foster deeper understanding and connection. Friendship fired with accurate empathy becomes companionship on life's journey. Opening their hearts within the embrace of empathic understanding, intimate partners grow deeper in their love and appreciation for each other. Families, groups, and communities seeded with empathic listeners can avert polarization and foster enduring connections.

Accurate empathy can indeed change you, opening your eyes and heart to the variety in human nature, to the diverse ways in which people are capable of perceiving and experiencing life. At the same time, in a mysterious way it also teaches the oneness of humanity— how in the words of the poet Carl Sandburg: "Alike and ever alike we are on all continents in the need of love, food, clothing, work, speech, worship, sleep, games, dancing, fun. From tropics to arctics humanity lives with these needs so alike, so inexorably alike."[31] Listening well and deeply tends to foster a compassionate and patient acceptance of human frailties—those of others as well as our own.

And here is a paradox, as so many truths tend to be. Something in most human beings reflexively wants to judge, correct, criticize, and punish shortcomings, as though we believe that people will change if only they can be made to feel bad enough about themselves. Yet precisely the opposite seems to be true. Feeling unacceptable invokes a kind of paralysis that makes it very difficult to change. Ironically it is when we experience acceptance as we are, a momentary realization of unmerited respect and grace, that change becomes possible. Gifted teachers and helpers learn how to provide such an empathic experience of acceptance for those they serve. Indeed, clients treated by counselors with high skill in accurate empathy are those most likely to experience positive changes, whereas low-empathy counselors can yield worse outcomes than no counseling at all.[32] The power of this kind of healing has never been limited to licensed professionals. It is possible to offer this gift to each other in everyday life.

Part of the gift is to "go first," to be willing to take the initiative and listen. It is a loving and contagious act to give your time and full attention by listening in order to understand. Being attuned to others is a choice that you can make in almost any situation.

Ideally the attunement will be mutual. Going first in listening is an alternative to self-centeredness that can open the door to mutuality and collaboration. This will not always happen, of course, but without listening attunement, meaningful relationship is unlikely to happen at all.

Empathic understanding can be a far-reaching choice. It is a way of being that rejects the illusion of us versus them. It is a step away from tribal thinking that envisions winners and losers, and toward an understanding of humankind as one diverse interrelated family. We are not required to do this, but our very survival may depend upon empathic understanding.[33]

Endnotes

1. Rogers, C. R. (1959). A theory of therapy, personality, and interpersonal relationships as developed in the client-centered framework. In S. Koch (Ed.), *Psychology: The study of a science. Vol. 3. Formulations of the person and the social contexts* (pp. 184-256). New York: McGraw-Hill.

2. Truax, C. B., & Carkhuff, R. R. (1967). *Toward effective counseling and psychotherapy*. Chicago: Aldine, p. 285. Italic emphasis in the original text.

3. I use the terms "empathic understanding" and "accurate empathy" interchangeably in this book, to refer to the broader ability that underlies the use of specific listening skills.

4. Gladwell, M. (2008). *Outliers: The story of success*. New York: Little, Brown.

5. Rogers, C. R. (1980). Empathic: An unappreciated way of being. In C. R. Rogers (Ed.), *A way of being* (pp. 137-163). New York: Houighton Mifflin. page 137

6. Gordon, T. (1970). *Parent effectiveness training*. New York: Wyden.
  Gordon, T., & Edwards, W. S. (1997). *Making the patient your partner: Communication skills for doctors and other caregivers*. New York: Auburn House Paperback.

7. Salzberg, S. (1995). *Lovingkindness: The revolutionary art of happiness*. Boston: Shambhala Publications; Armstrong, K. (2010). *Twelve steps to a compassionate life*. New York: Alfred A. Knopf.

8. See Note 6.

9. Reflective listening is a specific skill, and I use this term interchangeably with "empathic listening." It is also what Thomas Gordon called "active listening."

10. Rogers, C. R. (1965). *Client-centered therapy*. New York: Houghton-Mifflin.

11. Rogers, C. R. (1980). *A way of being*. Boston: Houghton Mifflin.

12. Aliberti, R., & Emmons, M. (2017). *Your perfect right: Assertiveness and quality in your life and relationships*. Oakland, CA: Impact Publishers.
Jakubowski, P., & Lange, A. J. (1978). *The assertive option: Your rights and responsibilities*. Champaign, IL: Research Press.

13. Wink, Walter. (2003). *Jesus and nonviolence: A third way*. Minneapolis: Fortress Press.

14. Cooperrider, D. L., & Whitney, D. (2005). *Appreciative inquiry: A positive revolution in change*. San Francisco: Berrett-Koehler.

15. Bass, B. M., & Riggio, R. E. (2014). *Transformational leadership* (2nd ed.). New York: Routledge.

16. Jung, C. G. (1976). *Psychological types*. In *The collected works of C. G. Jung* (Vol. 6), ed. G. Adler & R. F. C. Hull. Princeton, NJ: Princeton/Bollingen.

17. Myers, I. B., & Myers, P. B. (1995). *Gifts differing: Understanding personality type*. Mountain View, CA: Davies-Black.

18. Kiersey, D., & Bates, M. (1984). *Please understand me: Character and temperament types* (5th ed.). Green Valley Lake, CA: Prometheus Nemesis.

19. Berghoef, K., & Bell, M. (2017). *The modern Enneagram: Discover who you are and who you can be.* Berkeley, CA: Althea Press.

20. de Saint-Exupéry, A. (1943). *The Little Prince.* Orlando, FL: Harcourt.

21. Kurtz, E., & Ketcham, K. (1992). *The spirituality of imperfection: Storytelling and the journey to wholeness.* New York: Bantam Books.

22. Gottman, J. M., & DeClaire, J. (2001). *The relationship cure: A 5 step guide to strengthening your marriage, family, and friendships.* New York: Three Rivers Press.

23. [We were] made for joy and woe; And when this we rightly know, Through the world we safely go.—William Blake, *Auguries of Innocence*

24. Eldridge, K. A., Sevier, M., Jones, J., Atkins, D. C., & Christensen, A. (2007). Demand-withdraw communication in severely distressed, moderately distressed, and nondistressed couples: Rigidity and polarity during relationship and personal problem discussions. *Journal of Family Psychology, 21*(2), 218-226.

25. Rokeach, M. (1973). *The nature of human values.* New York: Free Press; Kirschenbaum, H. (2013). *Values Clarification in Counseling and Psychotherapy: Practical strategies for individual and group settings.* New York: Oxford University Press.

26. Miller, W. R., & Rollnick, S. (2013). *Motivational interviewing: Helping people change* (3rd ed.). New York: Guilford Press.

27. Franklin, B. (1772). Moral or prudential algebra: Letter to Joseph Priestly (September 19) *The writings of Benjamin Franklin* (Vol. 3: London 1757-1775).

28. A more complex version was described and studied by Janis, I. L., & Mann, L. (1977). *Decision making: A psychological analysis of conflict, choice and commitment*. New York: Free Press.

29. Miller, W. R., C'de Baca, J., Matthews, D. B., & Wilbourne, P. (2011). *Personal Values Card Sort*. Department of Psychology. University of New Mexico. Albuquerque, NM.

30. We used a similar card sort in a study of people who had experienced sudden transformational life changes: Miller, W. R., & C'de Baca, J. (2001). *Quantum change: When epiphanies and sudden insights transform ordinary lives*. New York: Guilford Press.

31. from Carl Sandburg's prologue to the 1955 book of photographs, *The Family of Man*.

32. Elliott, R., Bohart, A. C., Watson, J. C., & Greenberg, L. S. (2011). Empathy. *Psychotherapy, 48*(1), 43-49; Moyers, T. B., & Miller, W. R. (2013). Is low therapist empathy toxic? *Psychology of Addictive Behaviors, 27*(3), 878-884.

33. Miller, W. R. (2017). *Lovingkindness: Realizing and practicing your true self*. Eugene, OR: Wipf & Stock; Wilber, K. (2017). *The religion of tomorrow: A vision for the future of the great traditions—more inclusive, more comprehensive, more complete*. Boulder, CO: Shambhala Publications.

Made in United States
North Haven, CT
16 June 2023

37849927R00065